THE TOOLS OF GREATNESS

THE TOOLS OF GREATNESS

A Complete Catching Guide
Second Edition

Bobby F. Humphrey

Copyright © 2015 by Bobby F. Humphrey.

ISBN:	Softcover	978-1-5035-5156-5
	eBook	978-1-5035-5155-8

All rights reserved. No part of this book may be reproduced or transmitted in any form or by any means, electronic or mechanical, including photocopying, recording, or by any information storage and retrieval system, without permission in writing from the copyright owner.

Print information available on the last page.

Rev. date: 05/26/2015

To order additional copies of this book, contact:
Xlibris
1-888-795-4274
www.Xlibris.com
Orders@Xlibris.com
696035

Contents

Forward by Jim Thompson, New York Mets 7
Acknowledgements 9
Preface 11

Chapter One ------ A Catcher's Leadership 15

Chapter Two ------ Catch the Ball 20
                            Signaling, Receiving, Framing,
                            and Pitch Location

Chapter Three ----- Blocking—An Art Form 42

Chapter Four ------ Throwing 59
                            Focusing on Results

Chapter Five ------ Defensive Plays Around the Dish 89
                            Bunt Defense, Tag Plays, Double Plays,
                            Passed Balls, Pop Ups

Chapter Six ------- Note to Bullpen Catchers 115

Chapter Seven ----- A Coaching Plan 118

Chapter Eight ----- Evaluating Catchers 125
                            College Coaches' and Scouts' Perspective

Chapter Nine ----- College Recruiting and Catcher Film 133
                            Recruiting and College Baseball

Contributions 161
About the Author 163

Forward

By Jim Thompson, New York Mets

Catcher—the single most important responsibility of the position appears right there in the title. It is not the blocker of balls in the dirt or the one who throws out potential base stealers. We will receive exponentially more pitches during our playing days than we will be required to block or even throw. Regardless of the quality of our peripheral skills, arm strength, footwork, and ingenuity in game calling strategy, if we cannot catch, everything else becomes useless. Learning and honing all of the fundamental skills required of the position is integral to becoming a balanced, well-rounded defensive catcher. However, one skill stands above all of the others—receiving.

Catching is the most demanding position on the field. Physically it challenges our strength, endurance, and toughness. The catcher must have strong hands, a strong arm, plus the stamina to endure the heat of the season from a crouched position facing the opposite direction of all of his teammates. The catcher must fight through the nicks, bumps, and bruises associated with foul balls, jammed thumbs, and collisions at home plate. Emotionally and intellectually, the catcher must do more preparation than any other player on the field. He must learn the other teams' hitters and guide his pitching staff through the minefield of the opposing lineup. At times, he is a motivator, consoler, empathizer, or leader, and he must be unwavering in his desire to succeed.

The lessons in this book will serve as a guide for any catcher who wants to become well rounded and elevate his abilities. I once heard a coach say that catching is "the most over-coached and under-taught" position on the field. Coach Humphrey's book is the antithesis to today's trend of those who promise success through gimmicks, quick fixes, and shortcuts. Through his experiences as a player, coach, and his association with professional baseball, Coach Humphrey knows the requisite skills necessary to be a successful catcher. In the pages that follow, Coach Humphrey presents a framework and a plan that if followed, can improve your abilities.

Consistency separates the good catcher from his average or mediocre counterparts. Building confidence and consistency requires time and dedication; it will not occur overnight. Coach Humphrey presents each skill clearly and in a manner that is fundamentally correct, and when mastered, can lead towards the consistency needed to achieve at the next level. He starts with the foundation and builds upon it. Rest assured, there are no shortcuts or gimmicks. If you are able to master each of these lessons, the skills acquired will translate to all levels of baseball. Good Luck.

Acknowledgements

By nature, I am a thankful person, so it is nearly impossible to thank everyone that has impacted me in some way to eventually help make this book possible. From supporters to doubters, my gratitude cannot be measured.

From Little League through college, I was blessed with some of the best coaches—literally speaking—in their perspective levels. None was greater than my dad, Bob Humphrey, whom I shared many moments with, including my final game with Dad as head coach. A homerun blast to centerfield and a final handshake around third base was the most memorable moment of my athletic playing days. A tearful and on-looking mom finalized my step on home plate.

To my brother, John, I thank you for pushing me as a kid, making me earn it, rather than giving me an easy scoring chance in whatever sport we happened to be playing.

Special thanks to Coach Hank Burbridge, who was my head coach while at Spring Arbor University. His abundance of wins cemented his status as a Hall-of-Fame coach, but he demonstrated what was truly important as a coach, which has carried with me into my coaching career.

I would like to thank the hundreds of elementary students I have taught over the years, and especially my 2012-2013 class. Their high spirits and dreams helped motivate me through this process, which I shared with them daily.

Finally, I would like to thank some of the Spring Arbor Boys, all of which have taken leadership positions, undoubtedly using the life lessons learned as Cougars: Jordan Gruppen, Charles "Sale" Solaita, Tom Compian, Russ Gaston, and Seth Coffing.

Preface

I started playing catcher when I was in third grade. I don't remember too much about playing the position, other than I enjoyed it. Undoubtedly, I was one of the few players on my team who wanted to play catcher. It wasn't until the summer after sixth grade that I started to understand the importance of a catcher and what it meant to a team. During the first day of practice in sixth grade the head coach asked what position I played. When I told him catcher the bearded, brute of a man chortled and said, "You're my catcher!"

"If you're a catcher, your chances of playing at the next level are higher than any other position on the field." I first heard this statement probably as early as sixth grade. I started to understand its legitimacy when coaches never seemed to care how good I was, only that I was a catcher. From an early age, I was told countless times that my sure-fire bet to playing college ball was very simply that I caught.

This statement and notion, however, is one that drives me absolutely crazy! Being a catcher does not result in immediate or certain success. Being a *quality* catcher is what actually increases the chances of moving on, and there's a significant difference in quality and merely playing the position. As I continued my playing career I generated a level of pride and arrogance about the position, but it wasn't because I was necessarily that great at the position; I was passionate about it. Lazy catchers who didn't hustle on and off the field, or those who didn't block the ball offended me while I was still playing. Being a catcher, in my mind, was (and is) like being part of a distinguished group that represents leadership, toughness, knowledge and workmanship.

Little has changed now that I am involved in the game in a different capacity. I know that the catching position is not for everyone. Often times there is little glory. Catchers take a beating. Not only is there little glory, but sometimes unwarranted blame is placed on the catcher. We always hear the phrase, "Catchers are like the quarterback of the team." This is absolutely true, but what exactly does it mean? It means that the catcher helps direct his team through positive leadership. It means that a poor catcher rarely results in success of a team.

With playing the position comes great pride and understanding. Rarely do you see a championship team at the amateur level without a terrific catcher. This book is designed for those with the desire and attitude to play catcher and for coaches who want to better their teams by strengthening their teams' defense and leadership behind the dish. It is for all who understand the importance of a quality catcher.

Using This Book

As with any instructional book, this book will include repeated and common drills, technique, style, and illustrations. Some of the age-old drills will be explained and demonstrated, while other styles will present different philosophies and advancements. Some of the explanations will be similar to those aspects learned during younger years, while others may be slightly less conventional and may differ from what you have previously learned and coached. Be it hitting, fielding, base running or pitching, as a coach, I work extremely hard in being **purposeful**, which will be an obvious and repeated pattern within the book's text.

One crucial aspect of catching that is absent in this book is pitch calling and the in-game mental aspects of the position such as tendencies and game progression. Rather than teaching a blueprint for calling a game, I want catchers to understand the importance of game situations, knowing specific batter tendencies, and pitcher strengths and weaknesses. It is easy to follow a chart, calling for given pitches in nearly every situation possible, but catchers must develop game-calling skills aside from a written formula. The single best way to achieve this is by playing the game.

Possibly the most important note to make while using this book is that players and coaches alike must understand that no book, instructional video, or coach can create the perfect catcher. Only the person catching can dictate their own success through hard work and determination. This book offers keys to that success, along with drills and fundamental understanding. When using the ideas presented in the book, it is imperative to do so with a purpose. For example, if a catcher is working on blocking drills, set a certain percentage that must be blocked correctly, or make it into a challenge with a partner or individually. To put it simply, never just go through the motions.

Chapter One

A Catcher's Leadership: "Guarantee what you can guarantee."—Hank Burbridge, Spring Arbor University

Some catchers are blessed with talent such as a rocket arm. Others have to work extremely hard to maximize their talents through long hours in the gym. Like any athlete in any sport, some catchers have qualities that are simply better than others'. There is one quality that tops any physical qualities and it's noted first with the intentions of making it a priority and not to be ignored.

Most coaches vary in their tolerance of different behavior, and it should be expected that catchers carry arrogance and confidence, but laziness, negative leadership, and a "me first" persona is unacceptable on *any baseball team at any level.*

Noticing the Catcher First

I continue to firmly believe that a catcher's attitude and leadership qualities are oftentimes opposing coaches', scouting coaches', and pro scouts' first impression of a quality or a poor team. While there are always exceptions, rarely do I see a great catcher on a team that displays poor class, fundamentals, and discipline. During pregame warm-ups, the catcher begins to set the standard and demonstrates an immense amount of information about himself and his team.

Pregame

It is mandatory for those that I coach to wear full gear with the exception of headgear when the typical pregame routine begins. A catcher is a positional player of pride and leadership, not a coach's shagger. Whether a catcher is receiving the ball for the fungo hitter, or working on bunting drills, he should always be dressed in preparation for the game. The idea of infield/outfield is not only to get loose, but to prepare yourself at game speed. The catcher is no different, and his energy begins immediately.

When the routine moves to plays at the plate, it is expected that all catchers are in full gear for plays specifically at home plate. *Headgear should always remain on at plays at the plate anyway, so be purposeful in your practice and pregame routine.* Additionally, during those plays at the plate, carry the play out! Do not receive the baseball and give a lazy "swipe" to simulate a tag play. Drop down to make the tag as mechanically coached. For force plays, if they're not fully carried out with throws to first, your footwork and proper receiving of the ball should be carried through. Have a purpose for everything.

In-game attitudes to abide by

1. Hustle: Be the first on the field unless you're on base or still putting your gear on—always.
    a. Hustle should always be guaranteed, including in-play situations. The team will likely follow your lead. Catchers are the first players on the field, and the first players off the field. The only exception is when a catcher is not yet in gear because of being stranded or making the final out of an inning.
2. Be on your pitchers' team.
    a. Some innings are long and it can get frustrating if the pitcher is giving up a lot of runs or having a difficult time finding the plate. Oftentimes the catcher must take balls in the dirt, but remember this: pitchers are trying to throw strikes. There is no room for showing him up and being clearly and visibly upset. It is the catcher's job as the leader to help the pitcher regain himself. This may be through firm words on the mound, but do not show him up to your teammates, the other team, or anyone else watching. Catchers can do this by hanging their head, lobbing the ball back, sarcastically shaking their head and other negative gestures. None are appropriate. Remember that leaders lead through positive example.
3. Umpire relationships are crucial
    a. It is imperative for a catcher to have a good working relationship with the umpire. Consistent

communication throughout a game can make a big difference in the pitcher's chance for success on a particular day.
   b. Before the game, firmly shake hands with the umpire, tell him your first and last name, and ask for his. His name is *not* "Blue" or "Ump". This is unacceptable and will not help build a positive relationship. Catchers are to call the umpire by their last name, or in some cases, their first names. This depends on your established relationship with the umpire. In the very least, it should be, "Mr. Umpire."
   c. How should a catcher let the umpire know he disagrees with a pitch? The first answer is simple—don't. The head coach is the only person to dispute a call, but there are ways to tactfully communicate with an umpire. Oftentimes I see catchers shake their heads, hold a frame for an extended period, or display other verbal and nonverbal displeasures. These are all highly inappropriate. Instead, ask the umpire if you blocked him from the pitch, or just ask if there is anything you can do to give him a better look. Be sure of *how* it is said, too. How and what is said go hand-in-hand. If when asking the above questions, the umpire shows sensitivity, back off a bit. Most umpires will appreciate respectful questioning.
   d. Finally, keep the ball off of the umpire. Do all you can to protect the umpire, and he will be your friend.
4. Be purposeful in your vocal leadership.
   a. We know a catcher is supposed to be a vocal leader, so to simply put it, **be loud**! In tense situations, work hard to have a positive tone. "Let's go," can

still sound whiney. You're part of the same team, so use your vocal abilities in a positive manner. If you feel it is in the team's best interest for you to "get into them," do so in the dugout and challenge them to step up. Never, however, point blame at them as if you're not a part of the team.
5. Throw the ball to second.
   a. It sounds simple, but we see it differently too often. Unless the catcher has a sore arm, fire the ball to second base at game speed before an inning. Keep in mind, it may be the only time a college or pro scout can get a pop time! It also displays continued enthusiasm and attitude. Finally, it can help your pitcher, too. If you're an effective thrower, teams will notice, and in turn it can benefit your pitchers' thought process in dealing with runners on first base.

In summary, be aware of who you are as a catcher. The amount of energy and the team's attitude is greatly affected by the catcher's character, work ethic, and attitude. Nobody would ever assume that a catcher is angelic and "soft". As mentioned, play with an edge, but understand your role. Many coaches and scouts who attend showcases and other baseball events notice the catcher *first*. In choosing between a catcher with leadership qualities or raw ability, most prefer the one who possesses a grand work ethic, coach-ability, and leadership abilities every time. When a catcher possesses a plus arm, quickness and the desired mental capabilities, you have a star.

A catcher's top *attributes* are positive leadership, superior hustle, and a great work ethic.

Chapter Two

Catch the Ball

Signaling, Framing, and Receiving

Receiving and framing is often looked upon as an easy physical trait of catching, which unfortunately can sometimes mean it's an overlooked catching trait. Like any tool in baseball, framing takes a significant amount of practice and experience, and it is much more than merely catching the baseball.

A catcher's first job is to catch everything—always.

First and foremost, a catcher's number one job is to catch any ball, thrown anywhere. This is a mentality that should be deeply instilled in all catchers, and it's not a cliché. The idea of catching every baseball thrown is much more literal than this. We all know there are going to be balls thrown so far out of the zone that the catcher cannot possibly catch it. My suggestion for these pitches: catch it anyway.

The ideas supporting this method are simple: catchers must understand their top priority, and more importantly, they must understand the mindset that goes along with this attitude will place no blame on the pitcher. Catch the baseball without an excuse and with ultimate high effort.

One baseball publication valued each strike at around .1 runs per game. If .1 is close to accurate, for every ten strikes won, a catcher has saved an entire run for his team. Over the course of a season, one can only imagine the impact this has on a team's win/loss record. The best catchers in the Big Leagues may win around five pitches, or save around a half run per game. During an MLB season, that number grows to 81 runs per season. While these numbers may be rough, they do give some insight into the impact of a good receiver. Conversely, a poor receiver can be detrimental to a team in the same aspect.

It is important that a catcher takes pride in his receiving skills. Like many other baseball skills, receiving is an action based on timing. The glove must arrive to the ball on time in order to give the umpire a good look. When a catcher appears to be catching a ball that looks heavy and shows little control of the glove, timing is often the root of this problem. As timing improves, the catcher will be able to receive the ball with subtle glove movement, working close pitches into the zone. As a general rule, catchers meet the ball to the point of receiving. This will help catchers better understand the idea of "sticking" the ball (reviewed later) in the strike zone. Not meeting the ball to its zone will allow for the glove to be pushed out of the zone. Additionally, meeting the ball to its point allows for subtle arm movement into the zone. This is especially important for throwing-side pitches. Meeting the ball to its point will allow the glove to move slightly into the zone on those pitches that are just an inch or so outside—win pitches!

Pitching In a Zone

There are many different variations in coach-to-catcher pitch calling. Coaches give signs to the catcher to indicate the pitch type and the desired location. Coaches should use what is most comfortable for them and what is easiest to convey to a catcher. Following is a chart that may help in determining how to call pitches. Furthermore, when a coach wants his catcher to call a bullpen using certain guidelines, he can create a simple sheet for the catcher to follow. Rather than saying, "Fastball up in and in," they can refer to it as shown below. Each numbered location is called for each given pitch, and it does not change based on the hitter. For example, a "one fastball" is a fastball high and inside to *both* a lefty and a righty. Follow the pitch calls and the chart:

One fastball/secondary: A pitch thrown high and inside.

Two fastball/secondary: A pitch thrown low and inside.

Three fastball/secondary: A pitch thrown low and on the middle of the plate.

Four fastball/secondary: A pitch thrown low and outside.

Five fastball/secondary: A pitch thrown down the middle.

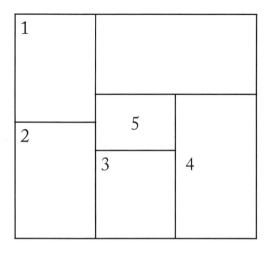

Key Points

A five pitch is also considered a "BP" (batting practice) pitch. These pitches are used in a lot of in-game situations. Some of them are as follows:

1. The pitcher is struggling to find the plate.
2. The batter is relatively weak and the coach wants him to "earn it", so he will "go right after him" to ensure he is not walked.
3. In a typical fastball count, it may be a good idea to throw a "five curve" right over the plate. If the pitcher has excellent command of his secondary pitch, it may be appropriate to call a five curve in a 2-0 or even a 3-0 count. In these counts, the batter is almost always looking for a grooved fastball. Even a curve right over the heart of the zone can make a batter buckle.

The blank, or unnumbered area is an area very rarely used when calling pitches. Seldom does a pitcher want to intentionally throw high and outside. Only in a very specific scouting report do we throw in that location.

Why?

High, outside pitches are the easiest to handle. As a batter, you hit outside pitches deeper in the zone, allowing the ball to travel further. Because of this, from the loaded position, the bat does not have to travel far, allowing for an easier pitch to make contact with. A mere flip of the hands can result in contact.

This is the opposite of pitches high and inside, often the hardest pitches to handle. The bat head has to travel further and quicker than an outside pitch. For inside pitches, the batter makes contact at the front of the plate for a faster reaction.

Calling Pitches

The mechanics of calling pitches are pretty basic. Taking a look at **Figure 1**, this photo illustrates very plainly how to sign pitches to your pitcher.

Figure 1

Feet Placement

This is really the only time a catcher should be on their toes. Be sure that the catcher's right leg is closed enough so that the first base coach cannot see the signs. It is most appropriate to point the knee toward the second baseman's play area.

Glove Placement

The catcher's glove should extend past the left leg, resting comfortably; put the wrist against the knee. This takes away any visibility from the third base coach. Do not place the glove inside of the left leg, and do not place it below the left leg. When giving signs correctly, there is no need to use the glove to shield below the legs. The glove is only used to be sure the coach cannot see *around* the left leg.

Hand Placement

Hand placement is the most crucial component of pitch calling. Notice two specific hand locations in **Figure 1**.

1. The hand is up high enough so fingers are not dangling below the catcher's leg. The fingers should never pass catcher's body. To be certain of this, simply place the wrist tightly to the waistline.
2. The catcher's hand is tight to his body. Any extension could cause others to see the signs. Keep the signs close to the body.

Giving Signs

Following the above basics and mechanics will allow for adequate pitch calling. Especially when more than one sign is given, be sure the signs are appropriately visible to the pitcher. Signs should be given briskly, but going too fast could cause for the pitcher to miss signs or not see them entirely. Simply be sure that all fingers are placed when giving the signs in a specific or unspecific sequence. If the pitcher is still having a hard time picking up signs, use your own creativity such as adding paint to the catcher's nails or taping fingers to be sure they stick out.

Runners on Second Base

The most common, universal method for calling pitches with a runner on second base is using the second sign in a sequence of signs. While this may work, it is important to change "hot" signs or sign sequencing. It could be the first sign, the last sign, or signs can change—this simply depends on the *catcher and pitcher's ability to communicate clearly*. Another common signaling sequence is "outs, plus one." The "hot" sign depends on how many outs there are. If there are no outs, the first sign will be the pitch called, and when there is one out, the second sign is the pitch being called. Finally, with two outs, the third sign would be the called pitch. Both catcher and pitcher must be on the same page and mentally strong when mixing signals. Being "crossed up", or not knowing what pitch has been called is entirely the pitcher and/or catcher's fault. *Finally, make certain the pitcher does not come set until all signs have been given! They should remain in the stretch until the entire sequence has been given.*

Framing and Receiving

A catcher's first priority is to catch the ball. This cannot be established, repeated, and understood enough. After this priority, when framing, the catcher's job is to help the pitcher win strikes. **Figure 2** shows the basic receiving position. Notice that this catcher is no longer on his toes, rather he is flat on his feet. In a standard receiving position the feet should be shoulder-width apart with the toes facing outward slightly. It is important that catchers do not receive the ball on their toes. This limits balance and the ability to move tremendously.

Figure 2

Body Placement

As catchers mature and become more advance, it is appropriate to begin inside or outside, and move as the pitch is being delivered. This can help deceive the batter and make him guess the pitch placement before the ball is delivered. For most, it is best to *slide* into the position. Catchers absolutely do not hop into position; this creates too much movement and sound, and can easily give away pitch location. Quietly and steadily moving into place with little movement is most sufficient. While the catcher's body placement will change slightly, depending on different variables, basic methods are as followed:

1. For inside or outside pitches, center the body and glove directly behind the black portion of the plate. The black should "divide" the catcher's body and the glove when centered appropriately.
2. For low pitches, it is appropriate to show a low target, but it may be more effective to simply motion the glove toward the ground. Be mindful of this during some counts when a ball thrown in the dirt is expected. Get the glove down, obviously reminding the pitcher.
3. High pitches should be indicated by the catcher's **glove**. Standing for high pitches can take away the umpire's view. Much like motioning for low pitches, motion for high pitches, and/or keep your glove at the desired location.
4. Have as little movement as possible! Moving around too much for the ball can tell the umpire that the pitch was clearly out of the zone. Keeping the ball in front of the body is important, but do it as subtle as possible. It's not always bad to reach beyond your body for inside/outside pitches, but lunging shows the pitcher missed the zone.
5. It is not necessary to put the throwing hand behind the body. Resting the throwing hand near the right (or throwing) ankle is sufficient. This helps promote balance on both sides of the body.

Framing

Think of cleaning a square picture frame. The same types of hand movements are very similar to catchers receiving the baseball. It is best to always catch the ball with the *fingers facing slightly upward or toward the pitcher*. To complete the analogy, the bottom of the frame needs little cleaning; the catcher's palm will rarely face up when correctly framing. Another analogy to help players understand is to imagine a steering wheel. The same basic mechanics and hand movement should be used when framing.

Move the glove when framing, not the arm! Pulling a pitch back into a strike zone almost always results in a called ball! Win pitches!

Target

As read above, catchers begin to move around a bit more at advanced levels. Because of this, there often isn't a defined target given to a pitcher. Following **Figure 2**, this shows a basic target for the pitcher. The palm is slightly down with the fingers pointed toward the pitcher, and the target is roughly knee high. Showing the entire mitt to a pitcher will disable adequate movement. *Good framing equals comfort.*

Movement on the Pitch—BEWARE!

Catchers are taught to begin the target low in the strike zone, which is where pitchers most often locate their pitches. In the picture, we see the target, which is about knee high to the catcher. As a coach, be aware of movement on the delivery. Even at advanced levels, including top-tier college programs, catchers have a tendency to allow their glove to rise on the pitch. This means the target may begin at the knees, but as the pitcher is in his delivery, the target ends up being essentially down the middle. If you are finding that your catcher cannot rid this habit, explain to him that he must force his glove downward.

Catching the Ball—Glove Movement?

Some teach to slightly close the glove upon receiving. I have no opinion on this, other than I want my catchers to catch the ball and frame it correctly. Adding too much to such a basic idea isn't always wise. Additionally, as catchers grow, subtle movements upon receiving the ball can help win strikes. As the ball hits the glove, "stick" it with a quick movement into the zone, but do not pull it with the entire arm.

Glove Side Pitches—Figure 3a

First, notice in the picture where the catcher's hand position is. It will change very little on any pitch. The fingers are positioned comfortably and naturally slightly upward—if the thumb is facing up, simply turn it towards the body, but NOT the entire hand. The only glove movement from the target is a simple turn of the wrist inward. A method to consider is to think about showing the umpire the baseball. Very little wrist action is needed, other than *turning the glove*, not bending the wrist back toward the body.

Figure 3a

High Pitches

Catching the ball with the fingers pointing toward the pitcher will "show the ump the ball". When pitches are high and inside/outside, use a combination.

Throwing Side Pitches—Figure 3b

Very much like inside pitches, be sure not to have too much wrist movement. Work on showing the umpire the ball. When framing arm-side pitches keep the fingers pointed toward the pitcher. If the palm is facing the pitcher, it can be difficult to frame because the baseball will force the glove out of the zone. Work to have strong hands, and show the umpire the baseball.

This location is typically the weakest. The catchers have to work to stay under the baseball, preventing the glove from riding out of the strike zone. As a rule, keep the thumb under the ball.

Figure 3b

Low Pitches

It is always best to catch with the fingers up. If it is necessary to catch the ball with the palm up, it is almost always out of the strike zone. On fastballs, it is difficult to stay under the pitch and keep it within the strike zone. This takes repetition and strength. Using a pitching machine to focus on low pitches can help with this. You can also try weighted balls to develop the appropriate muscles. *Work to stay under the baseball. The glove should never hit the ground unless the pitch takes the catcher into a blocking position.*

Stick the Ball, or Not Stick the Ball?

Some catchers are taught to catch the ball extended away from their body, "sticking" the ball out front. Others are taught to let the ball ride deep into the strike zone, catching the ball close to the body. Which one works best? Both can work.

I almost always have my catchers "stick" the ball for various, important reasons already mentioned. First, and most important, catchers frame pitches for the umpire to see well. As we have said, win pitches! Allowing the ball to ride is an acceptable method of framing for some (but not all) breaking balls. The idea is to allow a breaking ball to complete its break by traveling just a few inches further. It is best to stick almost all pitches.

The catcher's most important job is catching the ball! Remember to be comfortable, remain athletic, and have the ability to move quickly to pitches out of the zone.

Framing Drills

The best drill for framing is to catch pitchers! While it may seem mundane and redundant, it is imperative that catchers continue to work on framing while catching bullpens and other pitcher/catcher drills. Simply catching pitchers is absolutely the best framing drill.

It is also effective to practice framing while playing catch. The catcher does not have to be in a receiving position to work on correct glove action. Another option for all of the drills explained is to use a weighted ball. This will help strengthen muscles and also promote proper framing.

Practice receiving all pitch types. If on average you receive 60-70% fastballs in a game, then you should practice receiving the same amount. The rest of the time should be spent on working on drills receiving curveballs, sliders, changeups, etc. This varies from level to level.

Finally, practice framing from the secondary/throwing position. It is easy to neglect the secondary position with practicing receiving drills, but it is equally—if not more—important. Each catcher must become comfortable receiving from the secondary position.

Reaction Drills

There are various types of reaction drills, which focus on the idea of "catch everything," and framing is not required. This drill can be done with multiple people, or just a feeder and catcher.

1. The catcher remains in a normal receiving position, without his glove. He is faced toward the pitching mound.
2. The coach or feeder begins on either side of the catcher and rapidly tosses balls to the catcher, walking in a semicircle, around the catcher's front side.
3. The catcher catches the ball, and tosses it back quickly, ready to receive the next ball.

4. The feeder throws the balls to all locations, making it as difficult as appropriate for the catcher to catch balls from a normal receiving position.

This drill can also be done in a group. Catchers stand in a semi-circle and toss balls at the catcher, one at a time, in a left-to-right sequence.

Another drill to promote reaction is to have the catcher three feet from a wall, facing the wall. The feeder stands behind the catcher and tosses balls against the wall. The catcher reacts to each ball and its location, catching the ball. Tennis balls work best for a firmer bounce.

Partner Pitch—Figure 4

For this drill, no gear or glove is needed. With another catcher, squat roughly three to four feet apart. Simultaneously toss the ball underhand to the other partner. Receive and frame the ball as you would in a normal situation. Be sure to practice purposefully and effectively, working all locations. The receiving stance, hand and wrist action, and arm movement should be simulated as it would be in a game. This is a great drill to begin any catcher practice with. It is quick, easy, and if done correctly, very effective. *Alter secondary stances.*

Figure 4

Inside/Outside Drills—Figures 5a and 5b

This is a drill that primarily works on inside and outside pitches. As illustrated in **Figures 5a and 5b,** this drill is done with just one other partner. Each partner takes a turn throwing to its other partner from side-to-side. The partner on the left will receive the ball on his glove side to demonstrate an inside pitch. The partner on the right will receive the ball on the right side to demonstrate an outside pitch. After several throws, the partners switch.

Figure 5a

Figure 5b

Figures 6a and 6b shows a modification of the same focus. When there are three people, two are the throwers. The thrower to the catcher's right will place the ball on the catcher's glove side, and the thrower to the left will place the ball on the catcher's throwing side. This may be a more adequate drill to get more repetitions. Be purposeful in the drill and work hard to develop proper receiving skills.

Both of these drills risk purposeful repetitions. It is important that catchers stay balanced and maintain *correct mechanics and fundamentals*. The thrower must throw the balls accurately so the catchers do not have to make unrealistic lunges or create other positions.

Figure 6a

Figure 6b

Show the Ball Drill

As an attempt to get catchers to understand and/or feel the proper receiving technique, ask them to receive and show the pitcher or coach the entire ball in the glove. This also emphasizes down to up action, while allowing them the opportunity to learn by feel, instead of relying on technical instruction. At times, they may think they are showing the coach the ball, but they are not. During these times, verbalize to them when you (the coach) can actually see the ball. Feed the ball and have the catcher frame normally, but before dropping the ball, they are to show it to the person feeding.

Umpire Drill

Have catchers be umpires during receiving drills. Encourage them to discuss what they see from their teammate's receiving technique. If done in a healthy way, this constructive criticism will usually stick with the catcher more than what a coach may say. After all, teaching and analyzing are the best way to learn.

Be careful to not do this drill during pen sessions. Catchers work framing, blocking, and secondary stances during pen sessions, which is enough. Most importantly, the pitcher does not need the distraction of discussion from the other catcher.

Rapid Framing Drill

A partner sets up 15 feet from the catcher, on a knee, and throws 30+ balls to the catcher. The catcher receives each ball, frames it appropriately, and drops the ball off to the side.

A catcher's number one *priority* is to catch the baseball.

Chapter Three

Blocking—An Art Form

We have now established a catcher's top priority. As a catcher, catching the baseball as a priority really goes without saying. It's an obvious notion, but never over-emphasized. The catcher's most important *ability* is blocking the baseball.

Blocking the ball in the dirt, especially with runners on base, can prevent runners from advancing, and possibly scoring. In the game of baseball, one lazy attempt at a blocked ball could be the difference in a win or a loss.

Blocking is also of the upmost importance to pitchers. When a pitcher has confidence in his catcher, it is to his advantage, and ultimately the team's advantage because he can throw all pitches without worry of advancing runners. Having the ability to throw runners out also helps pitchers, but if a catcher is a poor blocker it takes away from the pitcher's game. Pitchers and coaches must have confidence to throws balls in the dirt in various counts and situations in a game with runners on any base.

The following will describe and illustrate blocking techniques, fundamentals, and form. Blocking drills should be an important aspect of *every* practice and pregame warm-ups. Catchers can never do enough blocking practice to not only become better mechanically, but to also rid the "gun-shy" factor. Blocking will be automatic and instinctive when practiced adequately.

Blocking Mechanics

Figure 7 illustrates the basic blocking mechanics for balls thrown directly at the catcher. The catcher must be as big as possible with no holes in his body to allow for the ball to go through. Here are the correct steps to proper technique:

Figure 7

1. Notice that the catcher's head is down, with his neck tucked closely to his body. I note this first because of safety reasons. Catchers must keep their heads down to prevent exposing their necks to the ball. This is the most dangerously exposed area on the body.
2. The shoulders are cupped slightly. This helps prevent the baseball from bouncing to the far left or right of the catcher. Opening the shoulders can allow for deflection.
3. The catcher is bent at the waist slightly. This will help keep the ball directly in front of the catcher.
    a. Not bending at the waist will make the chest stick out, which will allow for the ball to bounce further away than desired, or to the left/right of the catcher.
    b. Over-bending at the waist can cause problems. As a catcher, it is important to stay as big as possible. The catcher is also unbalanced if bent too far forward, which can lift the glove from the ground, and slow down recovery of the baseball.
4. The glove is tight to the body, between the catcher's legs, and the free hand is behind the glove. The free hand goes behind the glove for protection, support, and balance. *Most importantly, the glove must stay between the legs when blocking—we do not try to catch balls in the dirt. Drive the glove into the dirt!*
5. Notice the catcher's toes are pointed outward. This promotes good balance and a solid frame, rather than having the toes on the ground.

Blocking Inside/Outside Pitches—General Overview

Most, including myself, have been taught to block the baseball "back to the plate" on inside and outside pitches. This is not a technique that I coach with as much emphasis as it used to be taught.

When a catcher turns his body so far in an attempt to block the baseball back to the plate, there are disadvantages he is creating. To the right or left, catchers should very simply block the baseball in front of their body. Squaring their shoulders to the pitcher is enough of a "turn" to prevent the ball from skipping away to the right or left, and it is not necessary to try to place the ball back on the plate.

On a pitch off the plate, if a catcher successfully blocks the ball to or just in front of the plate, the catcher has created a bad angle for ball recovery. For instance, imagine a baseball that has been blocked to a catcher's right (and usually throwing side). The catcher has placed the baseball to his left, and on the plate. When a runner advances, rather than picking the ball up in front of his body, the catcher must angle himself to the plate to make an accurate, strong throw to second base. *Baseball is a series of races, and this does not help the catcher win the race.* Here are some key points for blocking pitches off the plate:

1. Square the shoulders to the pitcher, or perhaps towards the shortstop or second baseman, depending on where the pitch is.
    a. One reason catchers are taught to block the ball to the plate is so his shoulders are closed off,

preventing the ball from skipping away. If the catcher stays in the same position he would block from behind the plate, it will allow the ball to bounce away. Squaring or facing the pitcher will prevent this.
   b. On balls far off the plate, it is still expected that the catcher square his shoulders to the pitcher. The over-exaggerated turn of the shoulders is appropriate for this instance, because physically he will have to.
2. Push with the inside leg and drive off into proper blocking position. Sometimes catchers are taught to jab step with the outside foot, then push off with the inside foot. It's more of a simultaneous motion than this. It is unrealistic to see a catcher jab, push, and turn their body.
3. Do not use the glove to push the body! The glove is there to block the baseball! Later, there will be drills to target this area.
4. **Block the baseball!** With runners on, nothing should change. Sometimes catchers are taught to "drag, step, and scoop" to help prevent a runner from advancing. This leaves too many holes. Additionally, good base running teams will be going in the dirt anyway. Block the ball.

Blocking the baseball takes an immense amount of hard work. Blocking drills should be part of every practice. Blocking balls thrown off the plate takes even more work, because simply knocking the ball down with the body is not adequate enough. The correct foot-work and body mechanics must be mastered to better help the pitching staff and the team.

Recovering Balls in the Dirt

How do you correctly retrieve balls in the dirt to prevent runners from advancing, or to quickly make a throw to second base? *You retrieve balls as quickly as possible in the way that suits the CATCHER best.* Catchers may try to pop up from their blocking position, back to their feet in a crouched position. This takes some work and can be difficult. If a catcher can do this quickly and with more effectiveness, do it—it's just that simple.

Coach with a purpose. With blocking a baseball in the dirt, the mechanics are pretty straight forward, and there are really no methods to be more effective. Recovering a dirt ball is a bit different. If a catcher, from blocking position, is quicker simply firing off their back foot, then allow it. Do not force the pop-up recovery method, especially because it can have its downfalls.

Retrieve the ball as quickly as possible. Allow instincts to dictate how a catcher will throw the ball to second or third base after it has been blocked. The pop up method may very simply be instinctive. But if it's not, there can be other problems that prevent a quicker throw. Forcing this method can be counter-productive.

1. After popping back to their feet, the catcher will have to reach for the ball. If the ball is not directly in front of them, this will create more body movement, slowing the throwing process down—baseball is a series of races.
2. Popping back up can also cause the catcher to be unbalanced.

3. Depending on where the ball is, the catcher may not be in good enough position to use his power leg when throwing to second base.
4. Retrieve the ball before looking for the runners. Do not take your eye off the ball. Gather it, then check for the runner.

Allow the catcher's ability to be utilized! Catchers must work—at all times—on being quick. After blocking the ball, if the catcher must stand to retrieve it, the body should still remain low to make the quickest throw possible.

Finally, do NOT "rake" the ball into the glove when throwing to second base on a recovery throw. Use only the throwing hand, grab the ball firmly and make a quick throw to second base with as little shuffling of the feet as possible. Just remember to stay in a low, athletic position.

Think of this as being similar to a pitcher fielding a bunted ball. When the ball is stationary, the pitcher is to reach for the ball and take one jab step toward the correct base. There is no reason to rake when the ball is not moving.

Blocking Drills

Note: Blocking drills cannot be emphasized enough. However, drills must be done correctly to be effective. It is better to have quality reps than quantity. If a catcher is too tired or confused to complete these drills with perfect technique and understanding, there must be appropriate intervention. This is no different than any other drill. In summary, hold catchers highly accountable for correct

fundamentals and mechanics. **There are many, many blocking drills, and the following will absolutely not cover them all, but all are extremely important for purposeful repetition.**

Throwers note: In blocking drills, the coach or partner will be either kneeled or remain standing. If the thrower is standing, it is best to back up to at least 20-30 feet. Anything close does not show a realistic ball angle from the standing position. The best position for the thrower to be in is roughly 15 feet away from the catcher, knelt on one knee. This will help for more accurate throws to work a particular skill and the angle will be more realistic, coming from the throwers ear-level. While there are situations for the catcher to not know the location of a pitch, most of these drills work a specific area, so the thrower must be consistent.

Bullpen sessions: Be sure that catchers focus on all work, including blocking, during bullpen sessions. More than enough balls will be thrown in the dirt with purposeful pen sessions, and allowing catchers to take this time off is not beneficial.

Simulated Positioning Drill

Especially for younger athletes, it may be best to have repeated positioning. Model the correct position and allow the catchers to get into the position on their own. Repeat, and speed it up, using a verbal command. "Block, receive, block, receive." This will allow for beginners to get into the correct stance without focusing on a thrown ball.

Gun Shy Effect

This drill is specifically for modeling mechanics and ridding a catcher from the "gun shy" effect. The catcher must first be in the correct blocking position. The coach or partner will kneel as discussed above and rapidly throw a large amount (20+) of balls into the dirt so they bounce directly at the catcher. Balls thrown to the left or right of the catcher should be ignored. The thrower may attempt to bounce the ball close to the glove, further away so it hits the catcher's mask, or near his arms. But the catcher does not move. The balls do not need to be thrown exceedingly hard, but should be thrown firmly, with absolutely no arc.

For catchers that turn their head or hesitate to block the ball correctly, this will help them gain a better feel for the balls as he uses his body. If balls hit their arms or thighs, it's something they must get used to. Catchers have to deal with pain; it's part of the pride of being a complete catcher!

Rapid Fire

This drill is only altered slightly from the above drill. The only added component is that the catcher will begin in *proper receiving stance*. Don't forget to be in correct receiving position—do not allow catchers to begin on their toes. The thrower, from the same position, will toss balls rapidly at the catcher. The catcher blocks the ball correctly and immediately goes back into receiving position. Once the catcher is in position, the next ball should be coming quickly.

The Tools of Greatness

Be sure the balls are thrown rapidly, as the drill should be difficult and serves as a strengthening drill, but the top priority for this drill is a 100% blocking rate and perfect mechanics. *If the speed is too fast for the catcher to achieve his goals, the thrower must slow his rhythm.*

Three Position Blocking—Figures 8a, 8b, and 8c

Figure 8a

Figure 8b

Figure 8c

This drill's purpose is to block all parts of the plate, again with good mechanics. The thrower remains in the same position and will throw balls to the catcher's left, center, and right side. While this drill should be done with some quickness, it will not be as high-paced as the rapid fire drill. Rotate through several blocking positions, as desired by the coach or catchers. The drill should be at least three rounds, or 12 blocks. Again, we are promoting strength and quickness, as well as proper mechanics.

Coaches' notes:

1. All balls should be blocked with perfect mechanics. Do not allow catchers to catch the baseball—they need to be blocked.
2. Be sure the catcher is squaring his shoulders to the pitcher. If the drill is being done without a mound in position, allow for another catcher or coach to be in the position behind the thrower. *While we do not block the ball to the plate, it is crucial that the shoulders are in good blocking position.*
3. Watch for catchers dragging their feet—remember, fire off from the inside leg!
4. These drills are not expected to be easy, but if the catchers are simply not able to get into proper position, either slow the drill or throw closer to the body. Bad drills equal bad habits.
5. For inside/outside throws, aim for the catcher's foot and throw roughly an inch off of it. This varies, depending on the catcher's ability.

6. All throws begin with the catcher set up in the middle part of the plate. Be sure they're in correct receiving position—it's about habits!

No Hands, Three Position Blocking— Figures 9a, 9b, and 9c

This drill is exactly like the previous drill, except the catcher's hands are clasped behind their back. There is no glove needed, and any balls that go through the "five hole" are acceptable in this drill.

There are two main purposes for this drill. First, catchers need to use their legs when moving, not their glove. Sometimes catchers want to use their glove to help push their bodies, and this will result in poor mechanics. We want to build strong legs and correct mechanics. *Second, we are focusing on continued development in getting the shoulders squared to the pitcher.*

Figure 9a

Figure 9b

Figure 9c

Coaches' notes:

1. This drill may have to be slowed down even more from the above drill. Catchers with weak or tired legs may not be able to do this drill as well to begin with. If this is the case, I suggest going back to regular three-position drill.
2. The distance off the plate will also vary. Having the hands behind the back will make it harder to square the shoulders. Because of this, it will take greater effort in getting them turned. Balls too far off the plate may be unrealistic, especially for beginning/younger catchers.
3. It is best to use tennis balls or another type of safety ball. Without mid-section protection, it is unwise and possibly unethical to use real baseballs. It has been mentioned that catchers need to understand that pain does come with the position, but unnecessary pain is counterproductive.

Drills, Drills, Drills

Coaches come up with drills all the time. No matter the drill you see, create, or desire, ask yourself its purpose, goal, and what will be developed. Here are some other drills in brief:

Pitching Machine Blocking

Use a pitching machine to get an exact location of a pitch to hit the ground every time. Be sure to set the machine at 60 feet to simulate correct distances.

Simulated Location Blocking

Location blocking doesn't involve a ball. It is simulated blocking and can be used just the same as rapid fire and three-position blocking. The coach either tells the catcher where he will block in a sequence or he points to a location. Balls can also be set up in front of the plate. Catchers move into blocking position without a ball being thrown. The emphasis here is strictly on technique. It helps the coach see specific areas such as shoulder turn, glove placement, and power drive from the inside foot.

Live Pitching, Non-Bullpen

The thrower backs up to 50-60 feet and simulates all pitches, including off-speed pitches. Various balls are thrown in the dirt at various locations.

**Make this a game or competition. Throw 20 balls to the catcher, working all types of receiving and blocking. Be the judge, and if a ball reaches the fence or is not caught properly, start the 20 throws over, have them do push-ups, or another competitive consequence.

Fungo Blocking

Some use this drill close to the catcher and high speeds, and I do not condone that particular drill. It is dangerous and serves little purpose. However, during fungo-batted balls, a catcher can stand in the infield and move his feet as an infielder before setting up in front of the ball and blocking it with good mechanics. This, too, serves little purpose other than simply getting a feel for balls off the body. It does not promote correct footwork and mechanics, other than strictly the blocking position. The catcher should block the ball towards the fungo hitter.

Closing Thoughts

We have now covered the top three aspects of a complete catcher. A catcher's top attribute, priority, and skill set will promote an excellent team player and defensive catcher. Blocking the baseball is so extremely crucial, and if a catcher simply cannot or will not block the ball, a position change is needed, especially at the varsity level and higher. It is a skill that should be engrained and instinctive. Encourage the catcher to take pride in his blocking ability. Under his hat, suggest he has two tally mark categories that include throwing runners out and blocked balls. Any ball successfully blocked in the dirt will result in a tally.

The number one catcher's *skill* is blocking the baseball.

Chapter Four

Throwing

Focusing on Results

All aspects covered in this book are important, and absolutely should not be neglected, but we have now covered the three most important characteristics of a quality catcher. A catcher's ability to throw the ball with velocity, accuracy, and little movement is also part of a complete package. Throwing the baseball includes correct mechanics, but it is more about getting the ball from point A to point B, rather than a perfect stance, release point, and footwork. This is an aspect of the game that should be taught very much like hitting. If a hitter can get on base successfully at a high rate, coaches will not attempt to fix a swing that isn't broken. If a catcher can receive, block, and throw the ball to second base well, very little should be fixed or altered. In throwing runners out, it's about quality results, not perfect form.

Throwing at the catching position is all about timing and consistency. This involves the feet, legs, arms, and hands to be working in-sync with quickness and controlled precision.

While a big part of the arm strength component is God-given, the timing of the footwork portion can be improved significantly to make a remarkable difference when throwing out an attempting base stealer. Furthermore, a catcher does not need above average arm strength to be an above average thrower. An above average thrower has consistent technique with his footwork, exchange, arm action, and release point.

Important Coaching Tip—
Arm Action and Arm Angles

Catchers used to be taught to "throw from the ear", and this is no longer a stressed skill. Because of the transfer, footwork, and release location, the catcher will naturally throw from *near* the ear. However, baseball players are rarely taught to change arm action and this is for very specific reasons, mainly injuries. When asked how catchers should throw the ball, my response is unchanging and very simple: Just throw the baseball. Coaches will work with catchers to make quicker throws, but this does not have to be "from the ear", because by natural mechanics, they will throw properly. The same principles are coached with pitchers. Arm action is only changed for very well-thought reasons. Repeated arm action, landing points, and balance is much more important! Through drills and repetition, arm action changes naturally and safely.

While still not often changed, arm *slot* (over top, three quarters, side arm, submarine) can be altered slightly, but this should also be taken with caution. Catchers should do all possible to throw over top because it creates the straightest throw. Some catchers have an extended arm slot, placing the ball far from the body and very high *after* receiving it. I do encourage working with catchers to assure the arm is 90 degrees to the ground if they have an over-extension. But once again, if the arm is not at exactly 90 degrees, but the catcher is natural and productive, allow it. Otherwise, catchers typically have a natural short-armed motion. When extending the throwing hand too far back, it is creating more time.

Look for production, not form.

Throwing Runners Out at First Base

When the runner is getting too big of a secondary, and/or the defensive play calls for a back pick, throw the ball as quickly as possible. It sounds simple, and the concept is:

1. Throw the ball at the bag, not at the first baseman.
2. Catch the ball, explode out of receiving position, and reposition toward the target.
   a. This takes practice and repetition. A strong throw cannot be made if the catcher's feet are not positioned toward the target.
3. It is also effective to throw from one knee. Drop the left leg while opening to first and throw the ball.

Throwing Runners Out at Second Base

"Get your butt in the air! Higher!" I was taught by various coaches and through camps that there was one stance for properly throwing runners out at second base. We expanded our base. We put our throwing hand right behind the glove, gently touching the leather. We were also preached to raise our butts in the air, making for an extremely unnatural, uncomfortable, and prohibitive receiving stance. This isn't too far off proper mechanics, but I was told countless times to perfect this "stance", not my throw to second base. I always felt this made it harder to receive, frame, and block adequately. Things have not been altered too much, but the philosophies have gone back to the very first point of throwing to a base—do it as quickly as possible.

Different stances can be adjusted for comfort and quality of throws. The principles do not change, but preference may. This is up to the *player* first. When the individual needs altering, make the next step.

Basic Throwing Stance—Figure 10

The most recommended receiving stance to throw a runner out is shown in **Figure 10**.

1. The base is widened slightly. Be certain that the base does not take away the ability to catch, receive, and block the ball. Comfort is important, too!
2. The left foot is slightly in front of the right—the right toes can be inline with the left heel or the left arch.
3. Raise the butt up slightly to be sure your weight is not falling back.
4. The throwing hand can rest comfortably behind the glove, near the chest protector.

Figure 10

Throwing to Second, a Simultaneous Movement—Figures 11a, 11b, and 11c

When I coach catchers, I like to use the word explosive. The movement to second base is one that is explosive and quick:

1. Receive the ball first!
   a. Some have a tendency to leave the crouched position too early. This does not decrease the

time to second, and it can even slow it down. The exchange must begin immediately.
  b. The glove turns in the direction of the catcher's body, and the throwing hand reaches into the glove and brings the ball directly into the throwing position. Notice that the catcher's hand is already in the glove, ready to begin the transfer.
  c. The glove side has a big responsibility to stay on line and in a strong position throughout the throw. Think of a boxer's left hand and arm as he throws a punch; this is similar to the action of the glove.
2. Left knee cheat/collapse—**Figure 11a**
  a. Upon receiving the ball, the left knee will collapse slightly to begin the process and energy transfer.

Figure 11a

3. Right leg, short jab step—**Figure 11b**
    a. Be sure the step is on the midline, or throwing lane, to second base. The jab step creates stability while starting the energy transfer from the backside forward, to execute the throwing motion. *The picture is slowed down to best illustrate the jab step. In the actual process, the jab step is very powerful and quick. It's almost a "hop" step. Weight begins on the left knee and the short jab transfers the power.*
    b. Be sure the jab step is not too much. This will cause the arm to drag and slow the entire process down.

Figure 11b

4. Begin the throw—**Figure 11c**
   a. From here, the throw begins its entire process through completion. Focus on staying low and being explosive through the motion.

Figure 11c

Throwing Side Pitches Out of the Zone—Figure 12

Catch the ball. Throw the ball. In this case, it's basic body mechanics. Naturally, the body weight will already be placed on the right (back) leg. Reach, catch, and fire the baseball. To emphasize staying in place, catchers can "rock" slightly when receiving the ball. This helps to promote power from the back leg.

Figure 12

Glove Side Pitches out of the Zone—Figures 13a, 13b, and 13c

The same rules apply, in that the catcher catches and throws with quickness, accuracy, and mechanics. The main area of focus for glove-side pitches is how catchers receive the baseball.

"Hook" the baseball, do not reach. When a catcher reaches for the baseball, they must bring the glove all the way back, begin the transfer, set their feet, and throw. On glove side pitches, catchers hook the baseball and begin the transfer immediately. When hooking the ball, the body follows, lining the feet up to second base. In **Figure 13a**, the catcher is out of his receiving position because this is demonstrating a pitch out of the zone. His body is up because he is hooking the baseball before setting his feet.

Figure 13a

Figure 13b

Figure 13c

Differentiated Throwing Positions—Look For Quickness

It may be best to allow the catcher to remain in a standard receiving position. A couple of problems are often generated by not repositioning, however:

When a catcher's butt remains low, as in a standard position with nobody on base, the first movement in throwing to second base is often *up*. To generate the strongest throw possible, a jab step push-off is important. Because of this, catchers must fire *out* and up. The throw is a violent, explosive maneuver out of the catching position. When the catcher comes up first, they certainly do not have time to reposition for a strong throw, so it becomes an all-arm toss to second base.

Some catchers will remain low, but rotate their bodies. I have seen some catchers nearly parallel to the first base dugout, otherwise called a "side saddle" receiving position. It can create a very quick throw because, naturally, the catcher can get to the power position quickly. I do not recommend this type of positioning because it can create very poor ability to block the ball, especially to the left. Rotating slightly may be sufficient, and it is worth a try.

If pop time and accuracy can be improved, look to adjust:

1. The catcher's base. Look to see where his power leg is positioned. It may have to be exaggerated further back to get a stronger throw.

2. The catcher's butt. Raising the butt up may be necessary. When the catcher stands up when throwing, it's usually because he is not in an adequate power throwing position.
3. Ball transfer: Remember that the transfer begins immediately. Be sure the catcher is not putting his hand behind his back.

Most important questions to ask:

1. Can the catcher still **catch and block** the ball adequately?
2. Can the catcher improve their time to second base by repositioning or differing stances?
3. Is the catcher comfortable and able to remain balanced and quiet in the box (little movement)?

Throwing From the Knees?

Refer to the above questions. I almost always discourage this throw, and very few of even the best catchers even attempt this. It may be a quicker throw at times, but a catcher must possess a plus arm to make an effective throw.

When a catcher chooses to throw from the knees, it is a simultaneous action. As the ball is received, it is thrown as the knees move toward the ground. Catching the ball, then going to the knees before throwing will make for an even more difficult throw. As the body moves forward, release the baseball.

Coaching Tip

Be very mindful of throwing from the knees. It is done with a purpose, not to look cool or impressive. When a runner has a great jump, the catcher is attempting the very quickest throw possible. If the pitch is low, it *may* be best to attempt the throw from the knees, but this is very, very rare; the catcher must have superb throwing skills.

Delayed Steal Catcher Defense

When the runner at first base delays his steal, how should the catcher throw him out? It is natural for the catcher to simply throw as normal, but this can create problems, namely throwing power and defensive preparedness. Delayed steals are often attempted in a first-and-third situation. Upon receiving the ball, take two shuffle steps before delivering the ball. The shuffle will allow for a few things:

1. Balance collection: If the runner is not moving when the ball is received, the catcher will naturally relax. Remember, the catcher will already have the ball when the runner makes his attempt, so the throw does not have to be rushed. Shuffling, or re-balancing, will create a strong, accurate throw.
2. In addition, if there is a runner on third base, this will allow for a quick look to third to help "freeze" the runner.
3. Not only does the catcher relax if there is not a steal attempt, but so does the middle infield. They may also be taken by surprise, so shuffling the feet will allow adequate time for the middle infield to cover.

Coaching tip

Shuffling the feet will allow the middle infield to cover, but don't allow the middle infield to stay stationary anyway, especially with runners on third. Every throw back to the pitcher should be backed up by the middle infield, even when there are no runners on base. Keep players active and involved!

Throwing Runners Out at Third Base

Throwing the baseball 90 feet opposed to 120 definitely sounds easier, but there are obstacles for the catcher that include right-handed hitters and slow pitcher deliveries. Nothing should change in terms of positioning. Some catchers tend to relax more, assuming an easier throw. Don't! When throwing to third base, it is based on basic physics and preference. The transfer begins upon catching the baseball, same as any base.

Try hard not to throw over the hitter! Work on proper mechanics, remembering to stay low and move the feet. Catchers do not stand up and attempt a throw over the batter.

Basic Throws to Third—Figures 14a and 14b

Figure 14a

Figure 14b

For pitches inside, down the middle, or slightly to the right of a right-handed hitter, catchers are throwing behind the batter, not in front. Remember to receive the baseball first then begin the process of throwing to third base.

When balls are thrown within the zone (not reaching far to the right), a simple replacement step is used. The right foot replaces the left foot, the left foot makes a short step in line with third base, and the shoulders line up to third base. The catcher should already be deep enough behind the hitter that a drop step is not required.

For pitches that require an extreme reach to the right side, jab step with the right foot. As the exchange is made, the left foot comes forward, in line with third base, and the ball is thrown in front of the batter. The back foot (right foot) is used as a brace and push-off for strength.

Throwing Drills

As with receiving and blocking drills, use throwing drills as a progression. Each of the following drills promote arm strength, accuracy, and mechanics.

Throwing Drills—Catcher Specific

Keep in mind that throwing to second base requires a lot of effort; too many repetitions are unwise and can lead to arm issues. Not all throwing drills have to be max effort, and some do not even require a ball to be thrown.

Transfer Drill—Figure 15

Figure 15

With a partner, kneel 15-20 feet from each other. Show a target and have the throwing hand resting comfortably, as it would in real-game situations. Partners throw to each other and transfer immediately, in a game of basic catch. The transfer from glove to hand is the first movement before making a natural throw back to the partner.

Transfer Drill, Power Position—Figure 16

Figure 16

Back up to 60-90 feet and continue the drill from the power position. Throwing accuracy is important in this drill. If the catchers are struggling to throw the ball at each other's chest, shorten the length. The focus here is on the transfer still.

*This is the area when catchers with bad arm slots begin to change without any prompting or directing. Because they're focusing on a quick transfer and release, many catchers start to throw "more like a catcher". It's about repetition and muscle memory!

Dry Run

Practice the very basics of throwing to second base in this drill. Begin with a ball in the catchers' mitt and simulate specific steps as a progression. Use the explanation and illustrations for correct mechanics detailed previously in this chapter.

1. Work on basic left knee cheat/collapse only.
2. Upon receiving, simulate the right foot jab step several times without following through on a throw.
3. From the receiving position, put it all together and emphasize the explosive movement. Watch for the cheating left knee and small jab step. Go through all of the motions *without throwing the baseball.* Do this several times.
4. Go through the entire motion with a throw. The throw does not have to be to second base or thrown with high-effort velocity. Footwork and mechanics are priority.
5. Have the catcher work on everything from a thrown baseball. Again, high effort is not a priority.
6. Follow the baseball after the throw to stay in line.

Quarterback Drill—Figures 17a, 17b, and 17c

Figure 17a

The Tools of Greatness

Figure 17b

Figure 17c

This progressional drill will promote the idea of moving forward on a throw to second base. We want our power to be moving on a straight line to second base, and this will help develop the skill.

The catcher "drops back" five steps, just as a quarterback would, then shuffles his feet to the start position. When the catcher is back at the start position, they throw the ball to the partner, 70-90 feet away. When the ball is thrown, the catcher follows the baseball another 10 feet to help the feel of following the baseball in a straight line. Lengthen or shorten the distance if appropriate.

Reach Back Drill—Figures 18a and 18b

Figure 18a

The Tools of Greatness

Figure 18b

1. The coach or catcher stands behind the catcher's right (throwing) shoulder with the ball held out.
2. The catcher, facing second base, turns the upper body only and takes the ball with the throwing hand.

3. This will cause the left knee to collapse.
4. The footwork is engaged and a throw is made to the target inline with second base.
   a. To help promote a straight throw, the catcher can follow the throw.

This is a directional drill that keeps the catcher in line with second base on his throw and helps him feel a strong throwing position with his weight back.

Walking Line Drill

To allow catchers to feel all mechanics of throwing and drill these mechanics through repetitiveness, the Walking Line Drill is an excellent way to help with instinctive muscle memory and conditioning:

1. Begin at a location that will allow for ample distance, such as a foul line, or end line of a basketball court, if working inside.
2. A coach or feeder stands 15 feet away from the catcher, who begins in the secondary position.
3. The feeder throws balls to the catcher with enough velocity so that the transfer can be made easily.
4. The catcher receives and goes through the entire mechanical throwing progression with the exception of the throw.
5. Use the foul line to be sure the jab step is in line with the throw.
6. Repeat as appropriate. At the college level, going from the fence to a corner base is adequate in distance.

7. You can also use the Bounce Drill, as explained next, as an alternate to this drill. Rather than throwing the ball, bounce the baseball to the catchers to force them to stay back before throwing.

Bounce Drill

Catchers want to get a good start when throwing to second, but they must stay back to receive before the transfer process is continued. Watch your catcher closely, especially in live situations. If you are finding that he is coming up early, receiving the ball near his knees, try this drill, which forces correct mechanics. It must be done on a smooth, hard surface:

1. The coach will bounce balls in various locations (but within the zone)
2. The catcher will receive and make a transfer like normal, but will be forced to stay back and wait for the ball.

Closing Thoughts

All throwing basics have been covered, and it takes an immense amount of practice and effort, a common theme in perfecting anything! Leadership, catching the baseball, and blocking are the number one priorities of any catcher. A catcher with those qualities that can also place fear into the hearts of base runners is a stand out. Just remember:

1. Throw four seams.
2. Quickness is a focal point of executing most throws from behind the plate.

3. Mechanics cannot be forgotten—don't allow them to be neglected in any throw.

A Throwing Program

Each team has a throwing program, and while many are similar, teams adjust programs based on research, new trends, or use the basic long toss program. The most standard programs begin with throwers on a single knee, working back to high—not necessarily max—effort throws from an extended distance. Throwers then move in to finalize their program. Sometimes it's not quite that simple, but that is the basic model.

Watch teams as they warm up and go through their progression. At the collegiate level, you should see a variety of throwing programs within one full team setting. While programs may begin the same, each *position* has a routine or skill set to work on, even during normal warm ups. Baseball is a game of habits, and double play turns, quick hand simulation, and the like are practiced during a normal game of "catch." Keeping in mind the habitual and mechanical aspect of catching, I have developed a throwing program designed specifically for catchers, with **purpose** being its top priority—arm strengthening, mechanics, directional throwing. Below is a combination of throwing drills already demonstrated in this book in a progressional throwing program.

Use this program at your players' best interest! *This is not a blue print.* You will notice that there are no specific sets or distances given. This is to be determined by the players' levels, need, conditioning, and where they are in the program—mid season, offseason, summer. In parenthesis is a *suggested* throwing amount.

Step One—Knee Transfer Drill (10-15)

1. To begin the throwing program, use the knee transfer drill, demonstrated in the throwing chapter of this book.
2. The focus here is on the glove side turn, hand-to-glove as the first movement, and the overall transfer.
3. This also begins the warm up process.

Step Two—Power Position Transfer Drill (10-15)

1. At 60-80 feet.
2. Glove side turn, hand-to-glove first movement, and transfer.
3. Longer throws continue the arm program.

Step Three—Quarterback Drill (8-12)

1. 80-100 feet
2. Purpose now shifts to directional throwing.
3. Effort increases to promote arm strength.

Step Four—Normal Long Toss, A Change in Philosophy (8-15)

1. Standard long toss at 150-160 feet only.
2. 8-15 throws at high, to max effort—little to arc.
3. Normal arm action. Remember, we do not adjust arm action to "throw like a catcher." This becomes natural through the process of mechanical repetition.

Step Five—Deliberate, Mechanical Breakdown (5-10)

1. Starting at 150 feet, the catcher will go through each mechanical step in throwing, in a deliberate, slow breakdown.
    a. Knee cheat
    b. Right jab
    c. Throw and follow
    d. Repeat
2. Each throw should take the catcher closer to the target, closing the gap between throws. This is a mechanical focus, not an arm strengthening focus. Accuracy and mechanics are priority.
3. If two catchers are throwing, the catcher on the foul line should go through the steps, then step back to the original line. The catcher on the other end will continue his progression, stopping at 70 feet.

*Some rehab throwing programs have eliminated max distances that create those long, fence-to-fence throws with a lot of arc. Max distance is with high, to max effort, remaining on a line. Rather than using the model for just rehab, make it as part of the program. Most importantly, always remember that a throwing program is determined by what is best for the athletes, not a written formula of measurements and repetitions.

Chapter Five

Defensive Plays Around the Dish

Bunt defense, tag plays, double plays, passed balls, pop up priority

Any out in a game "could be" the most important. As athletes and sports enthusiasts, we are all guilty of assuming the game could be different if a certain play had gone the other way. This is true for any sport, and even when such stats and comments often annoy us, there's at least partial truth in all of them.

The following chapter will discuss many scenarios involving plays at the plate and proper execution of defensive plays for catchers. Each aspect will carry the same themes, which involve quickness, accuracy and execution, and safety. Every play at the plate can prevent a run from scoring. The one run could, after all, be the "difference in the game".

Bunt Defense

Coaching Tip

Who calls the correct play on the bunt? Generally speaking, most teams consider the catcher as the man in charge when calling out which bag to throw to on a bunt. It is assumed that because he can "see the whole diamond", it is the catcher's responsibility to call out the play. I encourage coaches to consider alternatives. Like anything, coach with a purpose, decide which works best for your team and philosophy, and roll with it. Should the catcher be the one calling out the play?

In bunt coverage, a lot of things are taking place. All positions—outfielders included—have an assignment and are moving on contact. What should be considered is that the catcher isn't simply sitting back directing traffic. The catcher is almost always moving on the play as well, and this can cause difficulty when a catcher has to make the correct call:

1. The catcher must decide if he needs to field the ball, possibly taking charge and calling off another positional player.
2. While considering whether or not to field the ball, the catcher must also scan the field to see where the base runners are. Can the team get the runner out at second or third? Or, is the only play at first base?
3. While fielding the ball, taking control over another position—or not taking control—the catcher must also see the entire play develop; he must then make the correct call.

Do what's best for *your* team—this cannot be said enough. But look at another approach, too. Have the positional players call the play. When bunt defense is executed well, specific players cover each base, and his job is to move to the bag and receive the throw from the other positional player. When several players are charging in for an attempt to field the baseball, they must react very quickly to a verbal signal. Consider having the positional player that is awaiting a throw at the base make the call. Doing so, it should be definite and distinct. The positional player at only third and second base will call for the ball. If there is no call, the ball is thrown to first base. The positional players at second and third can actually see the play develop better than the catcher. Try this approach and practice in-depth, then make a decision for what works best for the team. *Execution matters most!*

General Bunt Defense—Catcher

1. Do not hesitate to call off the pitcher!
    a. The pitcher is moving toward home plate. This means he must set his feet, reverse his momentum, and make an accurate throw. Be assertive and call him off to make the easier play. When the ball is up the base line too far, you're already taken out of the play and the other positions will call him off when necessary and appropriate.
2. Rake the ball into the glove?
    a. When the ball is moving, it is best to use the glove and "rake" the baseball into the glove with the throwing hand.
    b. When the ball is stationary, use the throwing hand only and do not take the extra time to rake it into

the glove. Baseball is a series of races, and if the ball is stationary it is much quicker to retrieve and throw with the bare hand.
   c. As a general rule of thumb, use an imaginary string from the heart to the baseball. At that point, the catcher will be directly over the baseball and in proper position to gather it quickly and make a strong, accurate throw.
3. Be sure the feet are set toward the target and assure accuracy—always.
   a. A ball thrown to the outfield is worse than a ball that is not thrown in time to get the runner out—remember this!
   b. Only in "do or die" situations does a catcher throw side-armed or off balance.
4. Always fire out of the catcher's box.
   a. This seems obvious, but the catcher must explode out to execute the play. When a catcher hesitates, or pussyfoots out it is usually because they're unsure if the play is theirs. Take control and fire out, assuming the play belongs to the catcher.

First Base Side Bunt Defense

Fielding a bunt toward the first base side is relatively basic. Field the ball and throw the ball, keeping in the mind the above notes. Be mindful of where the ball is hit. It may be necessary to create separation from the base line. It is a difficult throw to make around the runner, and it is just as difficult for the player on first to catch the ball over top of the runner. Again, only in "do or die" situations does a catcher rush the throw. If time is allowed, field the ball and take one hard step back from the line with the right foot, set the feet and throw. Remember to only rake when the ball is still moving. In most cases, grip the ball, set the feet, and fire.

Coaching Tip

For balls thrown to first base that are either bunted or third strikes in the dirt, the player covering first base must create a straight line for the catcher to throw to. Try coaching the player on first to actually get off the bag, putting their hands up, and preparing to receive. As the runner closes in on first, the player reduces the distance from the bag. If necessary, the player can put a foot on the bag if the play is going to be close. After receiving the ball, the player simply steps to first to make the out. Do not allow the player to be "married" to the bag.

Middle of the Field Defense

For any ball at the pitcher or just to the left side of the mound (pitcher's right), a banana route is suggested, just as outfielders would do. This allows the catcher to create an angle to first base. It may be more sufficient for the player to gather the ball then adjust their feet, rather than creating an angle. An over-exaggerated angle will waste time.

Third Base Side Defense—Figures 19a and 19b

Figure 19a

Figure 19b

When the ball is bunted down the third base side, a banana route or resetting the feet after gathering the ball is too slow. It is best to receive the baseball with the catcher's back turned to the infield. This needs to be practiced often to allow the catcher to understand where the ball is in association to where they're throwing.

1. Fire out of the catcher's box.
2. Overstep the baseball so the ball is directly under the body (imaginary string from the heart to the ball).
3. Use only the throwing hand to stick the ball.
4. Stay low and rotate the right foot so the left foot is aimed at the target and throw the baseball.

Basic Drill Work

The best method in practicing bunt defense is to do so live, in simulated game situations. Drills can vary in creativity, but there are a couple of basic drills:

1. Have another catcher or coach stand behind the catcher and toss balls onto the field of play. The catcher retrieves the ball and makes the throw, or sets his feet and simulates the throw. Standing behind the catcher will make it so the catcher does not "cheat" by standing up before the ball is tossed.
2. Put three to five balls in various positions, starting with the first base side, making a semicircle to the third base side. The catcher must start in receiving position, and on cue, they fire out and simulate making the play.

Tag Plays at the Plate

Tag plays at home plate can be tricky because they are high-intense situations. It is the difference between a run scored and a run prevented. If the play is tagged out, it can kill a rally and pump up the defensive team. A play at the plate can allow a team back into the game, tie it up, or take the lead. These high-stake plays are one of the very most exciting in baseball for the offensive and defensive team. Because of pressures, they can be hard plays to make.

Keep your mask on when plays are at the plate! There are various reasons to keep the catching mask on, but the first reason is for safety. While it is mandated that players slide at the plate at all levels other than professional, it isn't always the case. Catchers are the most vulnerable position on the field. Keeping your mask on will help prevent injury.

Figures 20a, 20b, and 20c show proper steps in making a tag play at the plate. Notice that before receiving the baseball, the catcher remains low. Infielders are taught to keep their gloves on the ground, rather than starting with their gloves up. This is true for catchers and plays at the plate. Be sure to be in an athletic receiving stance and start low. If the ball is not thrown in the air, it's hard to predict where it may go. It is easier to move up for the ball than it is to move down.

Figure 20a

Figure 20b

The Tools of Greatness

Figure 20c

1. The catcher can take *part* of the plate. If the catcher is blocking the entire plate without the ball, this is considered interference. Place the left foot on the left side of the upper half of the plate.
2. Upon receiving the baseball, drop the left leg to the back and side of home plate.
3. Keep the throwing hand *inside of the glove, gripping the baseball tightly.*
   a. This will help prevent the ball from being kicked out on a slide.
4. Drop the right knee down to cover the entire plate.
   a. The plate is now the catcher's once he has the ball. Be sure to block the entire plate and move appropriately if the runner slides inside or outside. Remember to keep the glove low to the ground to avoid tagging high.

5. Stay low. If the runner does not slide, provoking a collision, it is best for the catcher to stay low. By standing up and taking on the impact, it can cause injury or allow the ball to come out of the mitt.

Coaching Tip

Catchers need to be held accountable when practicing tags at the plate in practice and pregame warm-ups. Far too often we see plays at the plate not simulated. As mentioned in chapter one, catchers should always be in full gear, including headgear, when practicing or simulating plays at the plate. Carry out the entire action, not a weak "attempt" at a tag.

Close plays—Figures 21a and 21b

Figure 21a

The Tools of Greatness

Figure 21b

When the play is "bang, bang" at the plate, it becomes a simple reaction. A swipe tag may be necessary after collecting the baseball. When this is the case, simultaneously drop the left leg back and quickly swipe the runner at the plate.

Stay on the plate, or move off of the plate?

When the ball is thrown off the plate, do catchers move to get the ball, or should they stay planted and guard the plate? This depends on the situation and fundamentals of the team. With many plays at the plate, it is expected that the pitcher is backing up the catcher. The rest depends on the situation and score of the game, the inning, etc. If the run being scored is the winning run of the game, and you do not have time to collect the ball off the plate and make a tag, it's best to try to stay covering the plate and stretch for the ball. Essentially, it's common sense. Likewise, never allow the ball to pass if the run isn't as impactful. It may be more important to stop other runners from advancing than allowing one run to score. In these situations, move off of the plate and keep the ball in front—always. This is when the catcher must be mentally strong and understand all situations of the game before they happen.

Drills—Tag Plays

1. During all simulated plays at the plate, carry out the play.
2. Have a coach or another catcher stand in the infield and make a variety of throws to the catcher. Throw some off of the plate, bounce some, and change the situation. Practice "bang, bang" plays, too.

Double Plays

When I teach double play balls anywhere on the field, I emphasize "one plus one". This stresses the importance of making the first out before turning the double play. All focus should always be on the lead runner *if the situation calls for it*. Of course, if there is no need to get the lead runner, and the "easiest" double play is what is best for the game, then so be it. Most of the time, when double plays are turned at the plate they are crucial plays in the game. The infield will typically only be drawn in during must-do situations. As with all double plays, it is of extreme importance—most times—to get "one plus one" and guarantee the out at home plate.

There are two ways I teach catchers to turn double plays. Allow the catchers to work both styles and choose based on comfort, quickness, and effectiveness.

Figures 22a and 22b

Figure 22a

Figure 22b

Begin with the right foot on the upper half of the plate. Using the right foot, rather than the left foot, will allow for a little more mobility. After receiving the ball, push out to be inside of the diamond, and make the throw. Just as catchers do when throwing to second base, the transfer begins immediately after catching if possible.

Figures 23a and 23b

Figure 23a

Figure 23b

This method is similar to a double play turned by the short stop in a 4-6-3. The catcher begins moving toward the plate while the ball is being delivered home. When receiving the ball, the catcher drags his right foot across the plate, allowing momentum to move his body inside the diamond. The only thing that changes here is that the catcher is already moving toward the baseball.

Coaching Tip

Sometimes catchers feel "married" to the plate when doing the first method. Subconsciously, the catchers will stiffen up and lose mobility. It just happens. If your catcher seems to have difficulty moving to where the ball is thrown, or looks awkward doing so, try the second method. As the body moves, we become more athletic and this may help. Think of it as a preparation step for the infielders. We want them to be moving so they can better react on contact.

Be Aware

As with tag plays, there are do-or-die situations to be aware of, as well as situations when simply catching the ball is more important than getting the out. It may be necessary to keep one foot on the plate and do all possible to stretch to the ball. It depends—again—on the score and situation of the game. But catchers also need to be aware that allowing the run may not always be the worst-case scenario. Obviously, any time there is a force at the plate the bases are loaded. The catcher/coaches must understand and determine if one run means everything, or preventing other runners to move up is more important. Additionally, there is no back up for the catcher on double plays. A poorly thrown ball can result in two runs, and it can leave two more runners in scoring position. Simply put, be aware and understand all situations.

Passed Balls/Wild Pitches

The importance of blocking the baseball has been established as the number one skill set a catcher must possess. If the ball does make it passed the catcher, the next job is to get it back to the pitcher or the appropriate base as soon as possible. In the event the ball does get to the backstop, it is the catcher's job to get the ball back with as much quickness, accuracy, and proper velocity as possible. Follow the steps as illustrated in **Figure 24.**

Figure 24

1. Toss the mask. Getting rid of the mask in this instance is correct. Be sure to toss it far to one side so that it does not interfere with the play in any way. Avoid dropping it on or near the plate.
2. Slide into the ball regardless of what side of the plate the ball is on. Slide to the ball so that it is on the left side of the body. Sliding into the baseball allows the catcher to be more efficient.
   a. Bending over then standing upright to throw wastes time.
   b. Staying low creates a better angle for a potential play to be handled by the pitcher at the plate. By standing up, the catcher creates an angle downward. As the pitcher charges to home plate, this can be extremely difficult to handle.
3. Bare hand the baseball.
4. Come to the right knee and balance on the left foot.
5. The throw is from the ear, in a quick short-armed action.
   a. The ball cannot be lobbed, but it should be thrown with firm velocity. The throw is similar to throws in executing a run down. The positional players do not "load" in attempt to throw a high-velocity ball.

Coaching Tip

On all passed balls/wild pitches, encourage the catcher to slide into position. Even when there is not a play at the plate, the catcher can still be aggressive in sliding to the baseball and coming up in an athletic, strong position ready to throw to all bases.

Pop Flies

All baseball players at one time or another have been embarrassed by what looks like the simplest play in sports, the pop up. One of the difficulties in pop ups can be simplified relatively easily; defensive players must understand their fly ball/pop up priority and work together as a team to properly execute them. Infield pops practiced enough and should be a significant part of routine practices. *Communication and understanding is crucial in handling a batted ball in the air anywhere on the field.*

Catcher Priority

Catchers are correctly taught to catch absolutely everything they can—all positions are. Pop ups vary in height, so priorities are altered when necessary.

The catcher's actual pop up priority area is typically from the middle corners of home plate, back. Needless to say, if the ball is hit toward the first or third base dugout, the catcher is doing all possible to make the play, and/or support the pitcher, first baseman, or third basemen.

Coaching Tip

Don't allow the pitcher to be a spectator. The pitcher's priority/help areas include from the mound to the dugouts, and directly over home plate, and even behind the plate. Pops directly above the catcher are extremely difficult to catch. Additionally, pitchers must help the catcher in finding a pop up. The pitcher needs to be yelling and pointing to where the ball is. But don't allow a hit ball to drop because the pitcher won't field their position.

Catching a Pop Up—Figures 25a, 25b, and 25c

Figure 25a   Figure 25b   Figure 25c

1. Remove the mask, and do not toss it until the ball is found.
   a. Tossing the mask before the ball is found can cause problems. Toss the mask far away from the expected landing point so it does not interfere with the play.
2. The catcher turns their back to the infield. The ball will have a lot of backspin, and almost always move back

toward the field of play. Not turning your back will create an extremely difficult angle to catch the ball.
- a. Be sure to make every attempt to have your back to the infield regardless of where the ball has been hit. Think of it as an imaginary semicircle in the area of play.
3. Over exaggerate, if possible, getting back (toward the field) on a ball. It is best to be able to walk toward the ball and make the catch. Not giving enough room could allow the ball to drop behind the catcher, a catcher's nightmare. Be especially mindful of this when the ball is hit close to a structure.
   - a. Stay calm! Hurrying a catch on a pop fly often times leads to the ball dropping behind the catcher.
4. Don't stop playing defense. After the ball has been caught, be prepared to play defense, not assume the play is dead.
   - a. Some teams will tag a runner on first base, especially when runners are on first and third. A catcher thrown off guard can create an offensive play for the other team by a long, unaware throw to second base.

Against a Structure

Against a fence, wall, or another type of structure, it may be most appropriate to slide into the ball. This is better than rushing an attempt and bouncing the entire body off of the wall. Additionally, it gives a split second longer to make a catch. Be sure the legs are not stiff in this attempt, however—be safe.

Be sure to not give up on any pop ups. Pop up priority is based on angles and positioning. The first baseman has the proper angle to make an easier catch than the catcher when the ball is near the dugout, but all positions need to communicate!

First basemen and third basemen also depend on support by the catcher on pop ups in foul territory. The catcher is to communicate the player's position and if they have room. Direct verbal cues as, "Got room!" or "Out, out!" should be heard by all—be loud! **Additionally, line yourself with the baseball**. Do not remain stationary in the catcher's box. Rather, move to the baseball's side location to better support the fielder.

When do you practice plays at the plate? Plays at the plate do not come with a lot of drills because it's mere instinct! Coaches and players can simulate pop ups, double plays, tag plays, and other defensive situations, but the best time to execute and practice is during simulated games and scrimmages.

Backing Up First Base

Backing up first base is common at all levels, however it's not limited to just running down the first base line, attempting to beat out the runner. When backing up throws to first base, be reminded of two basic ideas:

1. Do not run close to the first base line. This is not a realistic backup point. Instead, angle toward the first base dugout or fence. If you run too close to the line, the ball will travel beyond the first baseman and the catcher! Decide an appropriate angle.

2. Yes, back up throws to first base with a runner on first. As the ball approaches the infielder, "drift" toward the backup location and see the play develop. Once the play is completed at second base, quickly move into the normal backup location. Don't be lazy; you could prevent a runner in scoring position by hustling.

Coaching Tip

Don't allow your outfielders to be spectators. Based on simple angles, it is not realistic for the catcher to back up all throws. Slow rollers, especially to third base, bunted balls to the pitcher, and essentially anything on the left side of the field could cause for a much longer run for the catcher. It is the right fielder's responsibility to move into a backup position *on contact*. When the ball is put into play, outfielders should be moving—*always*. Do not allow them to stay stationary!

Chapter Six

A Note to Bullpen Catchers

A bullpen catcher's place on a team is extremely important for a team's success. It is not a position that should carry shame, unimportance, or insignificance. Take the role seriously, because you're a catcher and a leader, and your time is coming!

Throughout this entire book you have learned instructional practices to make you successful behind the plate. When the time comes, if you're not the starting catcher, don't ignore the knowledge that has been placed. Prepare as the starter, even if your current role is to serve as bullpen catcher. There are many roles and purposes for a bullpen catcher, and it is not limited to warming a pitcher before the game.

Gear On—Always

When warming up a pitcher, in game or before the game, be a catcher! Leave the coat off, have all gear on, and work on blocking and receiving adequately. This also means being fully equipped when catching pitchers between innings. Wearing a coat, or a ball cap with a mask looks classless and sends a message of carelessness.

Coaches hate to wait! Bullpen catchers should also wear their gear *during the game.* Place your glove and headgear in a specific location as you watch the game, chart pitches, or other duties assigned. There are times in a game when a coach wants to make a quick pitching change with little notice. You should *never* have to waste time finding or putting on gear. When the time calls, get to the bullpen and wait for the pitcher. Any pitcher standing on a mound without a catcher is unacceptable.

First on the Field

If the starting catcher is stranded when the third out is made, you should be on the field *before the other team is off.* Same as above, you are in full gear, ready to play. Just as the starting catcher does, you are sprinting to your position, waiting for the pitcher to get to the mound. Even if the starting catcher has some of his gear on, get into position. You may not get a pitch thrown to you, but that is not of importance to you. You are there for the team and ready to warm up the pitcher.

It's About the Team

In chapter one, we discussed a catcher's mentality as a leader and the importance of a team-first attitude. Do not take being a bullpen catcher lightly. After all, you are demonstrating to the coach and the team what your attitude is, especially if you're disappointed that you're not the starter. It doesn't just start with being in the spotlight. The *team's* success doesn't start with only the nine players on the field, and you are an important part to your *team*.

Chapter Seven

A Coaching Plan

If at all possible, before a season begins, prepare the catchers through camps, clinics, or any off-season work allowed by your organization. Especially if they are new to the position, catchers need a lot of one-on-one direction. Do all possible to be sure catchers have an understanding of main concepts discussed in the book. After, catchers can begin a routine to do on their own during station work in practice. An in-season program depends entirely on team and individual needs. Much like lesson plans in a classroom, I don't approach positional work too far in advance. Let's try to stay away from cemented routines. Instead, create practice to simulate game-like drills as much as possible. Playing the game is the best way to learn the game.

During the season, framing and blocking drills should be done every day. This can be accomplished during station work or before practice. A catcher can never do too much catching and blocking. As mentioned earlier, do not allow catchers to neglect their catching practice during bullpen sessions.

Drills for all sports are typically progressional. Look for the very basic aspects of catching and evaluate your players' skill sets. For example, there may not be a need to do the "gun shy" drill found in the blocking chapter. This drill is designed primarily for those that are afraid of blocking. On the other hand, three position blocking may be too advanced—you decide.

Note For Camp Instructors

When players go to camps, the parents and the athletes expect to leave the camp better than they were when they entered. This can be accomplished, but it has to be conveyed to the player that it is *their* responsibility to continue success. As coaches working in time-limited environments, we are demonstrating, illustrating, and providing the tools necessary for players to continue their growth. Players won't leave better, they will leave with better *knowledge* to improve. Essentially, coaches will offer everything (and more) in this book for players to take on their own.

Catching Clinical Outline

The following is the exact outline that I take when I conduct catching clinics. Each point and drill is explained in the book, so use this book as a reference point. When I do full clinics, I alter them based on age. For ages below 12 years old, I do not necessarily go through each drill. As a coach, you must get a feel for what is appropriate. It takes me roughly three and a half hours to complete clinics, if done in one day.

I. **Introduction.**
   a. Introduce yourself as a coach, college background, etc.
II. **Taking away from this camp.**
   a. Responsibility is entirely yours.
   b. Work HARD so the drills are realistic and applicable.
      i. Coaches, feel free to assist to be sure they're working.
   c. Purposeful reps.
   d. Following this clinic, drills, and book will result in success. Catching is a weakness right now! Stand out!
   e. This clinic is not something for you to leave with as a better catcher. EVERYTHING presented needs to continue.
III. **Attitude and Hustle—Top attribute.**
   a. Noticing the catcher first.
      i. Catchers reflect the team immediately.
   b. Bad attitudes unacceptable.
   c. Never show the pitcher up—ever.
   d. First on the field, first off the field.
   e. POSITIVE leadership. You're not the coach.
   f. Umpire relationships.
IV. **Framing and Receiving—Top priority.**
   a. Signaling Stance.
      i. Glove, knee, wrist.
   b. Basic receiving position.
      i. Feet.
      ii. Glove placement (down!).
         1. Do NOT drift upward.
   c. Framing—picture frame/steering wheel.
      i. Arm side pitches a major weakness.

    d. Discuss subtle movements in the zone, inside/outside—meet the ball to its point, or BEAT the ball to its point.
    e. Drills.
        i. Reaction drill.
        ii. Partner simultaneous toss.
        iii. Three-person inside/outside framing.
            1. Weighted ball can be used.
        iv. Normal rapid fire framing.
            1. Weighted ball can be used.
        v. Umpire drill.
        vi. Discuss making it a game.
        vii. ALWAYS work framing—playing catch, BULLPEN.

V. Blocking—Top skill set.
    a. Can't block, can't play.
    b. Should be done as part of every practice.
    c. Basic blocking position (knees replace feet).
    d. Inside/outside blocking—not back to the plate.
    e. Drills—partner kneels, not stands.
        i. Verbal command (down, up).
        ii. Gun-shy drill.
        iii. Rapid fire.
        iv. Three position blocking.
        v. No hands, three position blocking.
        vi. Other drills.
            1. Game-like.
            2. BULLPEN—always.
            3. Pitching machine.
            4. Fungo? Do not condone unless ragball use. Can be good....if not dangerous.

VI. Throwing
    a. Results, not stance.

   i. Old school stance demonstration.
 b. Basic secondary stance.
   i. Straight toes, or:
   ii. Right toes to left arch.
   iii. Right toes to left heel.
   iv. Butt up slightly—about comfort!
   v. Hand behind glove, comfortably near chest protector.
 c. Throwing process.
   i. Transfer begins immediately. Turn the glove to the body.
     1. Player goes through 20 reps of only glove movement.
   ii. Left knee cheat.
     1. Repeat 20 times with glove movement.
   iii. Right jab step.
     1. Repeat all 20 times—put it together.
   iv. Glove has power responsibility—boxer.
 d. Review step-by-step process several times.
 e. Put it all into motion—explosive motion. Feel body move toward target. Catchers do on their own times ten.
 f. Walking line drill with coach as the feeder.
 g. Bounce drill demonstration. Explain bounce/line drill.
 h. Reach behind demonstration.
 i. Drills and throwing program.
   i. Transfer.
   ii. Power position transfer.
   iii. QB drill.
   iv. Long toss.
   v. Work back to partner, mechanical focus.
 j. Glove side—hook the baseball and throw.

k. Arm side, rock n' throw.
l. Throwing to third base.
   i. Replacement step.
   ii. Throw behind the batter.
   iii. Throw in front if the ball takes you there.
m. Pop times? 2 each?

VII. Defensive plays at the plate.
  a. Tag plays.
     i. Mask on.
     ii. Athletic receiving.
     iii. Catch, drop left leg.
     iv. Right knee to ground to cover plate.
     v. Ball in glove, hand on the ball.
     vi. Collision? Stay low.
     vii. Simulate plays—all areas (three throwers).
        1. Have a runner bear down but move to the outside! Get used to it.
  b. Bang-bang plays.
     i. Drop left leg and swipe simultaneously.
     ii. Simulate bang-bang plays with runner bearing down.
  c. Moving off the plate—discussion. When do you do it?
  d. Double Plays.
     i. Right foot, top of plate.
     ii. Push off to be inside the diamond.
        1. First baseman note (lining up).
     iii. Swiping double plays.
     iv. Again—sometimes it's a must do, other times you have to keep the ball in front. Be smart!
  e. Passed balls, wild pitches.
     i. Remove mask, toss.

        ii. Slide into the ball.
            1. Always, even with no play. Helps keep you athletics.
    f. Pop up basics.
        i. Turn back to infield.
        ii. Pop up area priority.
        iii. KEEP PITCHERS INVOLVED.

VIII. What do college coaches look for?
    a. Hustle and attitude. No player is indispensible. Bad attitude, and most coaches are walking away.
    b. Coach-ability. Are you eager to learn?
    c. Athleticism. We do not want fat, lazy catchers.
    d. Arm strength. Arm strength trumps mechanics because we can fix those. Throw the ball in warm ups! It may be your only look. If your pop time is slow but you have a strong arm, we will fix it.
    e. Blocking. Can't block, can't catch.
    f. Receiving.
        i. Generally a weakness. If you have some comfort, it's usually acceptable.

IX. Pro Scouts
    a. Discuss 20-80 rating system.
    b. Athleticism is top priority.
    c. Arm is a close second.
    d. Hustle and leadership (can help/hurt draft stock).
    e. Blocking and receiving.

X. Question and answer session. What can I help you with?

Chapter Eight

Evaluating Catchers

What do you look for as a college coach/scout? I get this question quite often. Sometimes the answer can seem redundant. "It depends." It really does depend on a variety of variables, but there are contrasts in the two. College coaches and scouts most definitely vary in prioritizing catching ability, but overall, there are musts to be considered at the college and professional level.

Pop-times are very similar to 40-yard dashes and fastball velocities. They're exaggerated like your crazy uncle's fishing stories, and they get better with time. Pop-times are used to gauge a catcher's throwing ability, but it should definitely not be the final test in grading a catcher. Don't allow it to be. To determine a catcher's pop-time, use a stop watch to time the ball from the instant it hits the catcher's glove, to the instant it hits the second baseman's or shortstop's glove. Below is a chart to better illustrate a scale for catching pop-times. These numbers are pop-times based on *consistent times*, not one throw periodically. Essentially, catchers that "live" at these numbers are scaled:

1.8: Elite, top tier
1.9: Exceptional
2.0: Good
2.1: Average
2.2: Below average
2.3: Poor

During my time in the game, I have seen *one* realistic, *consistent* 1.8 pop-time by an amateur catcher. This young man had an absolute cannon for an arm—probably upper 90's. Don't get overly carried away with pop-times, because accuracy is ultimately just as important, and oftentimes more important than the pop-time. Throwing runners out at second base is not a one-man show. The pitcher must be able to hold runners on.

Coaching Tip

When conducting pop-times, attempt to make them as realistic as possible. College coaches and scouts will time throws between innings, but we want to see live throws. Sometimes, however, that just isn't possible based on game situations. During practice, game simulation is a perfect time to evaluate realistic pop-times. When runners are on first base, mandate that they must attempt a steal within four pitches. This will give a clearer, more accurate time.

College Coaches Look For

In the book, I highlighted the most important aspects of catching as being attitude and hustle, catching the baseball, and blocking the baseball as the top three priorities. They *should* be a priority to coaches and catchers, but don't confuse that with the following priorities of scouting coaches and MLB scouts.

Hustle and Attitude

In chapter one I outlined the importance of hustle and attitude. Keep in mind that college coaches can replace a recruit or an already-existing player very easily! A coach can live with or without you, as a player. This is simply the cold, hard truth. A catcher that demonstrates poor sportsmanship can destroy an opportunity. There's always a coach out there that will take a risk or just doesn't care, but that is an exception to the rule and a rarity. As a catcher, get on the field, get off the field, and do everything humanly possible to not show negative emotion. As coaches, we want leadership, and we will walk away from a player with plus tools by a simple act of laziness or attitude. Keep in mind that this also includes situations of failure, such as striking out. While you're in the dugout, eyes are also on you. As already discussed, it is expected that catchers have an edge, but mere poor sportsmanship is unacceptable.

Attitude and hustle take no athletic ability whatsoever. Guarantee what you can guarantee.

Athleticism

If you're a catcher that displays work ethic and coach-ability, one can assume that if you're athletic, you can become an outstanding catcher. Coaches thrive off of those that are willing to learn, adjust, and welcome development. A young athlete with quick feet and the ability to move well in all directions is a wanted commodity.

Blocking Ability

See above. As a college coach, I look for catchers with the ability to block. While it is a skill of great importance, coaches have confidence in their ability to improve blocking skills. If you're athletic, you can block. If you're coach-able and athletic, you *will* block.

Arm Strength

Arm strength is God-given, but it is a must for catchers. As college coaches evaluate arm strength, there are variables to consider, beginning with mechanics. This is one reason we focus our attention to pregame, so throw the baseball! If we see sufficient velocity during pregame, we can make a quick determination if the catcher's arm is adequate for our needs. If a catcher has flaws in their mechanics while throwing from behind the plate, it can be disregarded based on what we saw in pregame, and it can then be written off that it's an area of improvement once the athlete is in college. Pure arm strength trumps mechanics in scouting.

Receiving Ability

Considering I outlined receiving ability and catching the ball as priority number one, this may seem a bit contradicting.

Generally speaking, receiving is a weakness for amateur players. Unfortunately, it is rare to see high school catchers with excellent framing ability. If a high school catcher displays leadership, athleticism, blocking ability, arm strength and the ability to win pitches, we have a stellar prospect before us. The only major issue that could occur here is simply a total discomfort in catching the baseball behind the plate. A lot of movement, flinching, and simply missing the ball will demonstrate incompetency in catching. But if a catcher shows basic comfort level and some knowledge of framing, it's usually acceptable. Nevertheless, refer to the book's entire contents to master all areas of catching.

I think the catcher's most important job is to keep the pitcher in his best rhythm. When I recruit a catcher, especially at showcases, I like to see which catcher is catching when a pitcher throws his best game of the showcase.
-Randy Mazey, Head Baseball Coach—West Virginia University

Professional Scouting

Scouting for the purpose of evaluating potential MLB players is a bit different in that scouts are looking *more* for God-given talent of the five tools. Attitude and hustle *does* play a role in evaluation, especially for "bubble players", or those players that are right on the edge of a potential draft choice. Scouts must ask themselves if players demonstrate a work ethic and attitude that would translate to an MLB club.

MLB teams use either a 2-8 or a 20-80 scale when evaluating the five main tools of speed, hitting, power, fielding, and arm. It is also used to grade various pitches. The basic, general scale is as followed:

80: Elite
70: Exceptional
60: Above Average
50: MLB Average
40: Below Average
30: Far Below Average
20: Poor

An 80 is rare for any tool. A 50 is considered MLB average. The following priorities for scouts are not necessarily in order of importance. To be considered at the professional level, it is expected that catchers posses *all* of the following. Essentially, it becomes a checklist.

Athleticism and Body

A strong, lean body is desired, with room to grow and continue to develop. Undersized or too heavy are turn-offs for scouts. They do not look for Greek gods, but a heavy catcher will break down a lot sooner than an athletic catcher. Demonstrating athleticism and quick feet is displaying to scouts that you have the ability to improve throwing and blocking mechanics, and quickness in fielding the position. It also shows endurance. The professional schedule is a long grind, and scouts are not looking for an out-of-shape catcher.

Arm Strength

A strong arm is a must. Throws to second base should have no arc. Throws should be between the waist and knee and on the left side of the fielder every throw. Throws should be four-seamed with little or no movement. Balls that drift, tail, or cut are not productive throws, no matter how strong. A weak throwing arm must be compensated by extremely quick feet and accurate throws. Generally speaking, arm strength is the first catching tool evaluated by professional scouts. When a player shows off a rocket arm, scouts pay close attention to everything else to begin the evaluation process.

Attitude and Leadership

It's a must. Poor attitudes and a lack of leadership can drop draft stock significantly. There is no blueprint, and each MLB team is different. See previous notes and refer to chapter one for general guidelines. In summary, be a leader.

Blocking

Catchers must be able to block the ball for all of the reasons discussed previously. There is room for growth here, but if catchers can block the plate well, they're certainly more attractive.

Receiving

College coaches accept a bit more rawness in this area than scouts do. Subtle movement, strong arms, and the ability to win pitches are priorities. Professional coaches will work to help develop receiving skills, but it will be expected that you're an excellent receiver coming into professional baseball. Win pitches!

From a pitching coach's point of view regarding catchers, they must first and foremost have dependable communication with each other. The catcher should be able to maintain a positive attitude and build confidence as he leads the pitcher through his entire outing. He must also be able to handle all types of pitchers with different types of pitches, including soft-throwing side-arm throwers, to over the top flame-throwers. The pitcher must trust the catcher's arm strength and accuracy to help control the running game. A catcher's blocking ability is extremely important to a pitcher, especially with runners on third base. This will allow the pitcher to focus on throwing his pitches, rather than worrying too much about base runners. Finally, understanding hitters' strengths and weaknesses and the ability to call a good game will contribute to success.

-Jeff Ware, Former MLB Pitcher and Current Pitching Coach—Yankees' Organization

Chapter Nine

College Recruiting and Catcher Film

Contents:

* Understanding the odds and three most important priorities
* Establishing contact with colleges
* Realistic understanding: What level is for you?
* Recruiting services
* Film preparation: Angles, reps, and useful film
* Player and parent-to-coach communication: Do and don't
* Integrity, professionalism, and desire—player specific
* Knowing the coach and the school
* College coaching red flags: Warning signs of a coach

And

* Private Instructors—are they worth the money?

Recruiting and College Baseball

Having played, worked with and around college coaches, and serving as a collegiate coach, I have always wished there was an informational piece to give to parents and players. Following is basic information about recruiting and college baseball. The views are mine with additional input from various college coaches, but they are shared by most. **Much of this information is very frank, but truthful.** Parents are included in the entire process.

In high school, I played varsity baseball with twelve players that went on to play college baseball—DI, NAIA, DIII, and Juco. These players were one year ahead of me, my graduating class, to two years below me.

Twelve.

Three played college baseball for four years, and two of them played professionally for a few years. Playing college baseball is an enormous commitment, and no matter the level, the workload increases dramatically. Unfortunately, some players are shell-shocked by the amount of conditioning, weight lifting, and required hours to improve the collegiate program. And one myth is lower levels, such as DIII, aren't taken seriously. Think again! As someone with professional scouting experience, I assure that DIIIs are not overlooked.

Playing college baseball is often a dream, but it becomes a dream because of successful years prior, or simple love of the game. To play any college sport, love of the game is not enough; it should be an infatuation, an addiction, a can't-live-without substance. As an athlete, you must understand:

1. You're not as good as you thought you were in high school. Being humbled is part of getting better. Every athlete, of every sport, of every level is humbled.
2. You better be coach-able and willing to learn from the coaches and leaders of the program.
3. You're not a shortstop, second baseman, outfielder, or catcher. You are a baseball player within that program. Looking at a college team, many athletic right-handed throwers were shortstops in high school. You will play the position that best helps the program win games and championships.
4. Personal stats previous to playing college baseball (and during, really) mean absolutely nothing to the coaches and upperclassmen.

Generally speaking, there are three things most college coaches look for in the order below, and it doesn't matter the given level. Obviously, various levels and institutions have different requirements and needs, but at their respected level and institution, priorities are as follows, in order of importance—hopefully:

1. **Grades.** Overall GPA, honors classes, and tests' scores mean more or less money and/or a safe recruit or a risk. Check your desired institution's acceptance rate and standards.
2. **Desire.** Not all great baseball players have the ability to play beyond high school, and oftentimes it is a lack of will and desire to work and compete. Essentially, coaches look at a player's ability *and* ask, "Does this kid have the work ethic to be part of my program?" That includes, many, many variables.

3. **Ability**. I strongly believe that there is a team for *almost* anyone with the academic strength and desire. Be realistic with yourself in goal setting. If you're stuck on "DI", you're limiting yourself. There are quality baseball programs at every level, and there is "DI" talent at every level. Conversely, there is sometimes questionable talent at DI. It's about the program, not a label. If it is.....**three...of twelve**. (Refer above) Ask yourself what is most important in your desire to play college baseball. Playing time? Elite status? Level? If you're content simply being on a team, there's a team out there. Numbers do not lie; an extremely low percentage of high school baseball players step onto a college diamond. If you truly want to play college baseball, be prepared for an honest evaluation and suggested placements.
    a. **Many athletes seem to be stuck on DI**. There are DIII, DII, NAIA, and JUCO teams that would run DI teams off of the field. I'm not speaking of top-tier, nationally ranked DI teams, and it's rare. Not all DI teams are the gateway to the majors, and there are players within the DIII ranks being scouted by professional scouts every year. If you have the potential to play DI, that's outstanding, but don't be married to the notion. College coaches will be truthful with you, so prepare yourself.

Getting Started

1. First, and foremost in importance, the responsibility to play college baseball rests solely on the athlete. High school and travel coaches cannot promise "full rides"

(which rarely exists in baseball, even at top programs), and it is the player's responsibility to be proactive, professional, communicative, and finally, perform.
5. There is no blueprint, so do your research. Not all colleges work the same way—a myth believed by many.
   a. Some coaches, especially at the highest college level, stick to specific travel teams and showcases, while also running college-specific camps—their own camps. Others use a variety of angles such as summer camps, clinics, showcases, etc. It depends on the program!
6. Be smart with how much money you spend. Attending camps and shoveling out thousands of dollars at a young age (or any age) is often useless from a recruiting standpoint. Target schools and go after them!
   a. Typically, the summer after the tenth grade is when DI coaches will start to target athletes. Baseball players sign DI letters-of-intent during the fall of their senior year, but they can commit at any time. Read up on NCAA, NAIA, and other organizational rules and regulations for contact requirements. **Even though LoI is signed during the senior year, scholarships are full long before that.**
   b. DIII schools will typically begin to collect a database, and they can recruit at any time, but most begin making a strong push during the summer prior to senior years. They can call and communicate with any age.
7. If you are extremely interested, *with the potential*, to play at a specific college, attend their camps if possible. If you're open to various schools, attend camps with multiple coaches in attendance.

8. Ask questions! Ask about camps and showcase teams, and do your homework. Some showcase teams promote the idea that they promise a scholarship, and that is highly unrealistic to promise. In fact, I would look at this as a red flag. I hear many complaints from parents that spend a significant amount of money for a showcase or individual tournament, and, "There wasn't a single college coach within sight." Just be careful; some showcase teams are business and money only! Fortunately, college coaches continue to learn quickly which travel teams develop and instruct players, teach fundamental play, and emphasize team play. Those that are more individualized are becoming more of a waste, and they're identified!
9. Look for small, intimate clinic settings. With multiple coaches but limited players, coaches can see everything they want in just a few short hours.

Using Recruiting Services

1. Recruiting services could be a tool used with great success, but your approach in emailing coaches and the communication you use is crucial. Basically, ask yourself: Why would a coach want to respond to my email or inquiry?
    a. Understand that coaches get many emails, sometimes one hundred or more a day.
2. Do your research, and be specific in your email.
    a. Sending generic emails to countless coaches is counterproductive. An email indicating that you feel you would "fit into the program," but having no knowledge of the program, institution, or

academic requirements will be exposed. Those emails, more times than not, are deleted.
   b. Look at the college, its academic programs, tuition, baseball program, the coaches, and more. When writing an email, direct it to the coach, and be "short and sweet." **Have another coach proof read it for you**.
   c. Call the coach as a second contact, and leave a voicemail that reminds him that you have sent video. After the second contact, wait for a response!
3. Be mindful of who you email. Especially for bigger, top-tier colleges, head coaches get hundreds of emails that go unchecked. Look to send video to the recruiting coordinator or positional coach.

Quality Video Film of Purpose

Sometimes video is very hard to watch because of its low quality, and sometimes it's not even clear which player to watch. Unless you have a professional-level tool that is eye-popping, coaches will not spend too much time watching video that is inadequate.

Game film? Game film can be boring and take too much time. Remember, you want to highlight yourself. Catchers and pitchers *usually* benefit most from game film. Hitting can be useful, but a coach can usually tell a player's potential by batting practice, using the guideline that follows. In summary, coaches do not want to watch an entire game on film. If feasible, coaches will come see you play at some point to see the overall player. Film should be looked at like a snapshot. "This is who I am. Come see the rest."

Infield: Include infield/outfield during pregame if possible.

Various angles can create a productive sample of infield ability, but stick with the following three if at all possible.

Recorder:

1. Straight on, from just behind the fungo hitter, or from the pitching mound area. This will allow the coach to see footwork, transfer, and release.
2. Behind the player. If, for example, the short stop is being filmed, the recorder will stand in the grass behind the playing area. This shows footwork, but more importantly, it shows arm strength because it allows the coach to see the flight of the ball.
3. Just behind first base. This view shows all of the above from a different angle.

Outfield:

Recorder:

1. Just beyond the infield grass. This will allow the coach to easily see footwork, release, arm action, and follow through.
2. Behind the fielder. This will allow the coach to see arm strength.

Catchers: Pregame warm ups are important!

Specifics are outlined on the following pages for catchers.

Pitcher:

Pitchers' film is sometimes hard to evaluate because the single most looked at tool cannot be determined—velocity. Most coaches must see a pitcher in person before determining their value. Film shows only mechanics and some arm speed:

Recorder:

1. Straight behind the catcher. This allows coaches to see command and secondary pitch movement.
2. To the opened side of the pitcher. This allows coaches to see arm action, landing points, and other important mechanics.

Hitters: The best time for a coach to see film of a hitter is during batting practice rounds. Live, in-game film helps, but a coach can determine tools and mechanics very quickly in BP. Approach, pitch recognition, and batter's understanding of the game is evaluated live.

Recorder:

1. **Straight behind the plate:** This is an important and often times neglected angle. This shows the flight of the ball, which can begin to show power potential. If

it's on a field or in a cage, getting behind the hitter is key.
2. **Straight in front of the hitter (opposite batters' box side):** This is where coaches will look more at footwork, bat angles, load, bat path, etc.
3. **Opposite base path side:** Moving in front of the hitter, and off to the base side will allow another look at the above batting mechanics while also seeing part of the flight of the ball.

Other Email and Person-to-Person Communication

Do and do not:

1. An "announcer" via parents is annoying when watching film. Coaches will not listen.
2. Sending stats and awards is ok, but does not give the big picture. Do not be naive to a coach's ability to know a given area and talent level. When coaches want a player, they do their homework. Stats are good, but don't rely on them.
3. News articles and paper clippings are for personal scrapbooks, not recruiting materials.
4. Some coaches are annoyed by basic grammatical mistakes, and it's not because they're English teachers. Sending an email riddled with errors indicates that you are not serious about your desire and you did not take the time to review what you're saying to what could be your college baseball coach. If you struggle with written expression, have someone edit it. That time spent assuring you sound professional is worth it.

5. **The player, not the parent, should email coaches!** Most parents think their son is a superstar, so the "rah rah" email about a parent's son will likely be trashed. It shows immaturity in the player and a lack of responsibility. Additionally, if the player is that serious about playing college baseball, they must show it every way possible—it's not *only* about the talent.
6. **Don't beg.** Sounding desperate is off limits.
7. Too many emails/calls can be counterproductive. If they want you, they'll call you.
8. **Parents and Players:**
    a. Under no circumstances should you ever put down a previous coach—Junior College, college transfer, high school, travel teams. Coaches do not want to hear it. It shows weakness and lack of accountability. That, "someone else's fault" mentality does not fly.
    b. Likewise, don't rip on previous or current teammates to a coach. In athletics, you have personal accountability and a team-first approach. This immediately creates questions for a prospective college coach: *What happens if he plays here? Will he throw us under the bus?* Additionally, many times it means one thing—envy. I have recruited players whose parents ripped professional draft-worthy teammates. It's sour grapes.
    c. Be cautious of bragging too much. "My son has played on a travel team since he was eight." That's useless information, especially considering everyone plays travel ball. Good information would include outstanding performance at elite showcases, so long as it's honest. Hitting a game-winning homerun in the state title game would be good information.

Integrity, Professionalism, Demonstrated Desire

Honesty Counts!

Let's keep one thing in mind: Coaches compete on the field and off in recruiting efforts. They want the upper hand and every advantage possible to beat their opposition, but don't confuse that with being enemies. While competitive in nature, many coaches within states, regions, or even conferences have great friendships and relationships. Coaches help one another by references, recommendations, networking, and the like. **Don't think for one minute that coaches do not communicate about recruits!** This is a hard subject to not get "preachy" about, but some players sink themselves by dishonesty. Be open and upfront with coaches concerning your potential decisions. It is then his job to convince you that his institution and program is the best fit for you. If a coach is offended that you have other options, that's a red flag in itself, and one that will be later touched on. I have recruited and heard about many recruits that take themselves out of a good situation because they're lying to various coaches. For programs with high moral and ethical standards, they will baulk, and eventually they will drop the player from consideration. There is always, and rarely with exceptions, someone else they can move on to.

Coaches also know signing deadlines, NCAA regulations, and the like. All of us have heard from a parent or player (usually the parent) that their son was "seen by" a top-tier program, so they're waiting for them to offer. If it's April of the player's senior year, there's no offer coming, and *all* coaches know this. That is extremely rare, and those late offers are typically for junior college transfers with a specific trait. This is a strategy parents use to prompt other coaches' interest. Usually, it's the opposite. As stated above, coaches are friends. It takes one simple phone call: "Coach Smith, have you seen Timmy play? Is he being offered?" This happens *a lot*. Be honest. If a coach asks what other coaches have contacted you, and nobody has, simply tell him! They see what they see; they're not using other opinions for their own program.

Have you been in trouble? What is your GPA? What was your high school batting average? How hard do you throw? What is your pop time? Most coaches dig deep. It's a lot like a job interview. Coaches would much rather you tell them the truth, even if the truth isn't stellar, than completely lie. As coaches do their homework, these questions will be answered. Understand that sometimes a coach will ask you the above questions, already knowing the answer.

First Impressions….well you know.

When a coach meets a potential collegiate student athlete for the first time, they don't expect a military-style haircut and a three-piece suit. But appearance usually matters. Many programs, public and private, have grooming standards where facial hair and long hair is not permitted. That doesn't mean that if you have either of those, the coach will write you off, but be aware of how you're presenting yourself. Long hair and facial hair can still look presentable. Be aware of dress, too.

Look them in the eye when they speak, and respond respectfully. Responding with "sir" can't go wrong. Coaches also know that young athletes sometimes lack in oral communication, but you must show interest. Looking uninterested or bored will turn a coach off instantly.

Desire

There is a fine line between begging, and overdoing it to get a coach's attention. Once you show interest, and do so with a purpose (remember those emails?), the coach will remember you, especially if you're presenting him with a team need. Desire isn't shown by over-communication and begging. Desire can be small things:

1. Do you call the coach back?
    a. You better! Until you have made your commitment, do not blow a coach off at any program. Be truthful and upfront, but listen to what he says and add that to your options, if you're fortunate enough to have them.
2. If you're interested in the program and there is mutual interest, do things promptly, such as sending transcripts, speaking with admissions, and other application processing items. If a coach has asked you to apply, and you're interested in the school and its program, I suggest having the application complete within a week. *Make a follow-up phone call to admissions to be sure they have received the appropriate material.*
3. At a game, go speak with the coach after. You know he's there (usually), so if it's within NCAA guidelines, approach him.
4. **During the game, your desire shines brightest. Character counts.**

Buying the Coaching Staff

You're not only trying to impress the coaches; the coaches also must impress you. When all signs point to a college, it's likely a great choice. **But remember that no college is perfect. Before engaging in college visits, list "musts." What must you have to attend the college?**

Considering the Coach's Interest:

1. Look for direct emails, letters, and phone calls, rather than generic invites to camps or what I call "filler" letters. Filler letters keep the institution in the player's mind, but it's not a serious, "We want you," letter.
2. Coaches will invite you to camps, and sometimes it truly is because they want to be able to see you and communicate with you in person. Be cautious of simple invites as mere money raisers. I suggest having your varsity and/or showcase coach review the letter and follow up with the coach. If they're sincerely interested, they'll respond very quickly to the coach. Some coaches do use their camps as a primary recruiting method.
3. Phone calls mean one thing—you're wanted. Emails serve a purpose, but a call speaks volumes. Check NCAA guidelines for when coaches can communicate by phone.

Ask the Coach Some Questions:
(Parents, you're included in this!)

1. What types of study halls are required within your program?

2. What are your social and academic expectations for the young men on this team?
3. Where do you see me (player)/my son within your program?
4. What is your coaching philosophy?
5. How do you motivate your team?
6. How do you hold players accountable on and off the field?
7. How accessible are you to the players during the offseason?
8. What are acceptable reasons to contact you?
    a. Not playing time and not philosophy. Don't bother.

These are just a few questions of many possibilities. Be careful, however of how you ask questions. *How you ask a questions is oftentimes more important than what you ask!* If a player or parent comes off as aggressive, that's a red flag to coaches. If they feel a player will likely be coddled or there will be issues, especially playing time issues, most will drop the player from consideration immediately. **Playing time will almost never be entertained, especially by parent request.**

Red Flags

I firmly believe that a coach is selling himself as a leader and his institution as an academic choice that provides growth and maturation for the future. Some coaches tend to go out of their way to bash another program or institution. Be cautious of this. I have always felt that this was an indicator that the coach was not confident in his own institution or competency as a collegiate coach. Some coaches do not get along, and some feel strongly about a university's downfalls. It's part of coaching. Look for coaches that, instead, deflect questions about another school to shed light on his:

"The University of 'Smith' is known as a program of partiers, and I have heard the coach condones immoral behavior. Is this true?"

This type of question can be hard, especially if it is true and the coach knows it. The best answer:

"I cannot speak on behalf of The University of 'Smith', but here at The University of 'Jones', we put high character as a priority within our program."

There are some gray areas here, and subtle reactions, pauses, or a simple yes shouldn't necessarily deter you. Just be cautious of those coaches that go out of their way to bash another coach, program, or school. There are coaches that will attack institutions for a variety of reasons. You should want to know about his school, not about another competitor. And don't mistake *facts* for belittling.

Facts, such as:

1. The opposing university is an outstanding college, but it has the same academic programs and accreditations for thousands less.
2. The opposing university has an outstanding coach and baseball program, but they have four catchers, when we have an opportunity for you to compete for playing time immediately.

3. The opposing university is ten hours away, and we're only two, so your family can see you play every weekend within the state.
4. Our school has state-of-the art facilities, while the other does not provide ample facilities to grow as a player.
    a. This one is used often, and it's warranted. Schools with outstanding facilities are attractive. It's simple.

These are just four varying examples of comparing and contrasting to sell their product and university. Facts, known facts, like these, are part of recruiting. Again, coaches should deflect, then *reflect* everything good about their programs!

If you have the grades, desire, and potential to play, enjoy it! Playing college sports, at any level, will provide invaluable experiences, friendships, and memories. The implemented hard work, loyalty, and dedication will prove to be significant in life after college.

Top attributes in playing college athletics:

1. Grades
2. Desire
3. Potential and ability

Most important communication reminders:

1. Be honest.
2. Be prompt.
3. Be professional.

4. Do not beg.
5. Players, not parents, make the first contact.

Private Instructors—a side note:

There is one true way to get better at playing baseball: Play the game.

A lot.

It appears that there is a somewhat new phenomenon. In our current society, it's no secret that people want success as immediate as instant coffee. Parents are dishing out thousands of dollars to have a self-proclaimed "expert" teach them how to hit their way to the professional level in just a few short hours, and oftentimes, that's a farce. College baseball players and professional players have spent thousands and thousands of hours (not dollars) working on their game—weight room, on the field, conditioning, batting cages. A few hours a month with an instructor is not the gateway to ultimate success on the diamond. They can help you, and they can also hurt—badly.

Fact: There are some outstanding academy owners and private instructors. They are there to help the community, and their involvement and instruction is truly beneficial.

Fact: There are private instructors that for some reason have received an unjustified label as a baseball guru, and they're hurting development for their personal monetary gains and pushing their own name.

Private instructors should aid development, but they are absolutely not where baseball skills are taken to the next level. So, the question becomes: How do you know if an academy instructor is worth the money?

Weeding out instructors:

First and foremost, don't be afraid to challenge them! Quality instructors, if as knowledgeable as they proclaim, should be able to give definite, specific ideals and reasoning behind anything they are coaching. Be it pitching, hitting, catching, or another area, they should be able to speak in-depth about the skill.

Example: If you're looking for an instructor to help you with a glaring weakness, let's say in the area of hitting, ask specific questions on how that instructor is going to benefit you. There are many areas of hitting that can contribute to unsuccessful at-bats. Working to fix a mechanical area should be a progression. It should also begin with any instructor speaking about an approach, **not attempting to perfect the mechanics of a swing**. When a hitter is struggling with a certain, specified area—lunging, opening up, wrapping the bat, casting his hands—a quality hitting coach will work through a progression. So ask an instructor: "My son is having hard time, opening his upper half, pulling off of pitches. What types of drills and mechanics will you present to help him?"

An answer to this type of question should be immediate, well-articulated, and reasoned with philosophy, mechanical insight, and a "let me show you" approach.

The bottom line is, don't dish out money to an instructor that sits on a bucket and exclaims, "Good," after every underhanded toss. Coaches everywhere have worked with players that have spent hours with personal instructors that have only regressed, and it's not due to philosophical differences; it's due to a lack of quality instruction. Are private instructors "wonderful" because they compliment all of the time and make you feel warm and fuzzy? No coach should completely tear you down, but if everything you're doing is "good," do you need the instruction? Is the instructor "good" because he is making gains, or is it because he's a salesman that is able to make it seem like the player is on top of the world? Maybe it's because he's providing that one-on-one attention that high school coaches simply cannot provide? The bottom line is, don't mistake empty praises for progress.

The questions are posed merely to get you to think about the instruction received. Quality instructors are factual and honest in your ability (without being complete jerks, of course).

There are outstanding instructors out there, but there's not one that can take your game to the next level, as often promised. That comes through hard work and playing the game. It's your responsibility and nobody else's.

Catcher-Specific Film for College Recruiting

The idea of sending film to college coaches, usually through internet video, is to give a glimpse of your skill set. Film is designed to show the coach the basics so he will then follow up with you to see you at a game or at his own showcase, if possible. Film should be relatively short, but it must be thorough enough to "sell" yourself as a worthy prospect that meets the needs of the team. Keep in mind that all coaches are different, but the following will discuss areas to avoid in taking film, and target purposeful, game-speed, catcher-specific areas to send to a coach.

Remember:

1.) Film should be short—four to five minutes, tops.
2.) Coaches get a lot of film, and they will decide very quickly if you're a worthy prospect.
3.) Oftentimes, coaches are able to decide within a minute if the player is a prospect for his program. The rest of the film is watched and repeated *if potential is seen.*
4.) Wear a uniform. Do not dress in typical gym-like clothing. If you can, I suggest using your high school jersey.
5.) Film must be as game-like as possible, even if it is not actually during a game. Pay close attention to specific detail in areas explained.
6.) A brief introduction is fine; keep it short and sweet. Explaining your desire to play college baseball and that it is your "dream" is wasted time. If it's not already written, the following information is appropriate
    a. School.
    b. Travel team.
    c. Graduation year.
    d. Test scores and GPA.

Avoid:

1.) Do not have someone sit on a bucket and feed balls to the catcher for receiving, and be cautious when doing so even for blocking. Anyone can frame pitches at low speeds from a coach sitting merely 15 feet away.
2.) Long periods of in-game film. Game film can be a useful tool, discussed in the following.
3.) Do not put pop times on the film! Coaches can very easily decide the correct, appropriate pop times from their desks.
    a. Do NOT write your pop times in any way on the film. Sometimes profiles list "best" times at 1.8 and lower. That is highly unrealistic. If a catcher is a true, consistent 1.8, *he's being scouted by professional scouts.*
    b. If you send a written bio to coaches, it needs to be accompanied by film. Again, stay away from stats; just show the coach.
4.) Being lazy! It happens, even on film designed to be sent to collegiate coaches.
6.) As said above, film should not exceed five minutes. Double play turns, bunt defense, and areas not mentioned in this manual can be seen live. Don't bother with them.

Framing

Framing is crucial and wins pitches, strikes, and runs. It is one of the single most neglected defensive skills on the entire diamond! Unfortunately, framing can look simple on film if someone is feeding baseballs to a catcher at low speeds, only a few feet away. This is not purposeful. Very, very few catchers demonstrate their framing skill in such a way that highlights their ability.

Live pitchers only!

An easy way to focus on framing is during a game, but that can take too much time, as there are delays in a game by way of foul balls, pitchers taking their time, etc.

Instead, use a bullpen and catch live. High velocity pitchers work best because coaches can see catchers' ability to handle trouble areas—low, throwing side, throwing side/low. The higher the velocity, the better because if the catcher frames correctly, it shows strength in meeting the baseball to its point of reception. Remember, catchers do NOT catch and pull into the zone.

**Move inside and outside. Do NOT sit up down the center of the plate. Show the coach that you know how to get into position.

Film Angles: Suggested—8 Pitches each.

1.) Behind the catcher, slightly to the left or right.
    a. This will allow for the coaches to see the pitch out of the pitcher's hand, all the way to the point in which it is received.
    b. Don't forget curves and sliders! Have the pitcher signal the pitch, just as he would a normal pen session. From a righty, those pitches are extremely

important to frame on the catcher's right side. Likewise, he has to show the same ability from a lefty if possible.
2.) In front of the catcher, on the right or left side.
   a. This view only shows the last couple of feet of the flight of the baseball. It will, however, show a little bit clearer demonstration of proper receiving abilities.

Blocking

During the framing portion, tell the pitcher that he should throw at least two pitches in the dirt, probably breaking balls outside.

Blocking film is pretty simple because if you cannot block, you cannot catch. It is important to block a couple of live baseballs, but this is a skill in which a thrower can stand relatively close. However, I oftentimes see a small number of balls blocked straight on, with no real speed. Camera angles absolutely must help enhance!

Film Angle—Nine to 12 blocked baseballs.

1.) There's really only one suggested angle—behind the thrower.
   a. The thrower will take a knee roughly 10-15 feet from the catcher. He will throw to the catcher's left, center, and right in sequence. This should be done with quickness, but be sure that it's not

necessarily rapid fire. Throw right, throw center, throw left, and repeat.

b. Don't cheat! Be sure to avoid moving left/right before the pitch has been delivered.

c. Being in front of the thrower does not allow the coach to see if the drill is being conducted appropriately, with firm tosses to make the catcher work.

Blocking is a crucial aspect of catching, but most collegiate catchers are at the very least adequate blockers. It seems simple, but this should be sufficient for coaches.

You can enhance framing and blocking by mixing up live pitches, but this can take too much time. Short and sweet is best, and the coach can see athleticism in blocking with this simple drill. Just be mindful to do so with quickness and *firm throws from the thrower*. Lazy, weak tosses are useless.

Throwing

Arm strength is a gift in terms of talent. Not all catchers possess what coaches would consider to be "plus" arm strength, but mechanics, athleticism, and quickness can overcome a lack of pure arm strength. Conversely, coaches are confident in their developmental skills, and if a player possesses a plus arm with poor mechanics, most are comfortable adjusting. When filming throws to second base, coaches will watch the mechanical process, footwork, and arm strength.

Before filming, take two to three practice reps in throwing to second base. Any more than that can create fatigue because throws to second are often max effort. Throws to second base consist of the following mechanic steps as a process:

1.) Transfer with a glove-side turn.
2.) Left knee cheat/collapse.
3.) Short, powerful, right foot jab step.
4.) Throw (hands are moving into throwing position during this simultaneous motion.)
   a. After the throw your body should be completely in line with second base—coaches will see steps moving out of line, often toward the left. This creates tail and can cause arm stress.

From each camera angle, throw three times.

Film Angles

1.) Behind the catcher.
   a. You can do this simply standing behind the catcher, on top of a chair, or in the stands if they're close enough. Be sure not to be directly behind the catcher because this is the angle that shows the flight of the baseball. Do not block this view. Coaches, if they wish, can get pop times here, or they can simply see the flight of the ball, which demonstrates arm strength.
2.) Directly to the side of the catcher.
   a. Here, the coach will not see the flight of the ball. He will see only the mechanics, looking for the previously listed mechanical steps.
   b. Avoid standing right in front of the catcher. This is useless.

The coaches' eyes are going to look for the power of the throw first and foremost. Catchers' arm strength is one of the first noticed traits, similar to that of a pitcher's fastball velocity. Coaches can quickly determine if you have the arm strength sufficient for his needs. This is why illustrated pop times are useless, and even annoying, especially if exaggerated. Let him determine and use his own watch!

Other areas?

Some film includes bunt defense, double plays, pop ups, and passed balls. Coaches will see plenty from a defensive standpoint by demonstrating the three primary skills of catching. Additionally, if you're sending hitting as well, film can get laborious when too long. Stick to the noted skill sets and let him determine if he should schedule a game live. And remember, leadership, character, and hustle trump all—be a leader.

Contributions

Many people helped make this possible, and I give many thanks to their support and efforts in helping.

Coaching Instructional Support

- Jim Thompson, New York Mets
- Mario Garza, New York Yankees
- Logan Mann, Southern Virginia University
- Marlin Ikenberry, Virginia Military Institute
- Randy Mazey, West Virginia University
- Andy Pascoe, University of Evansville
- George Laase, Valley Baseball League
- Ian Hearn, Michigan State University, Rockford High School, MI
- John Gehardt, Traverse City Central High School, MI
- Brad Balentine, Traverse City Central High School, MI
- Ricky Gregg, The Yard Baseball/Softball Academy, Roanoke, VA

Monetary Contributions

- John Sczykutowicz
- Flo Humphrey

Editorial Contributions

- Blair Hathaway-Johnson

Photos By

- Andy Vanhook

Catching Models

- Oscar Aguirre
- Bryant Hayman
- Michael Adkins
- Zachary Fisher

Field Use

- John Moxie Memorial Stadium

About the Author

Bobby Humphrey was born and raised in Michigan, and played college baseball at Spring Arbor University, where he lettered four years as a catcher. Since graduating, he has coached all levels with the exception of professional, including two years as a head varsity coach, one year in the Valley Baseball League, and numerous camps and clinics throughout the country. He has coached several players that have gone on to the college level and beyond.

Currently, Coach Humphrey is a collegiate coach, as well as an Associate Scout for the New York Mets, a position held since 2009. As a scout, he has evaluated numerous players to be drafted to MLB organizations, from top picks to late-round selections. Coach Humphrey is regarded as a top catching mind and his developmental work has been demonstrated by many in which he has worked with. He currently resides in central Shenandoah Valley, Virginia.

Mario Garza

Mario Garza helped tremendously in the making of this book, giving professional insight in various areas, namely receiving and throwing. He is currently a coach in the New York Yankees' organization, and works during the off-season and Spring Training with all professional levels within the organization. Garza helped co-write and revise the New York Yankees' organizational catching manual. After playing two years at Stanford University, Garza transferred to the University of Florida and completed his college career for the Gators in 2003. He then signed with the Houston Astros and played four years in their Minor League system before concluding his playing career in the Frontier League in 2007.

Made in the USA
Middletown, DE
16 July 2019